THE SPIRIT-FILLED MOTHER'S GUIDE TO TOTAL VICTORY

THE SPIRIT-FILLED MOTHER'S GUIDE TO TOTAL VICTORY

Harrison House, Inc.
Tulsa, Oklahoma

The Spirit-Filled Mother's Guide
to Total Victory
ISBN 0-89274-908-3
Copyright © 1994 by
Harrison House, Inc.
P. O. Box 35035
Tulsa, OK 74153

Published by Harrison House, Inc.
P. O. Box 35035
Tulsa, OK 74153

Presented to

_____

By

_____

Date

_____

Occasion

_____

Contents

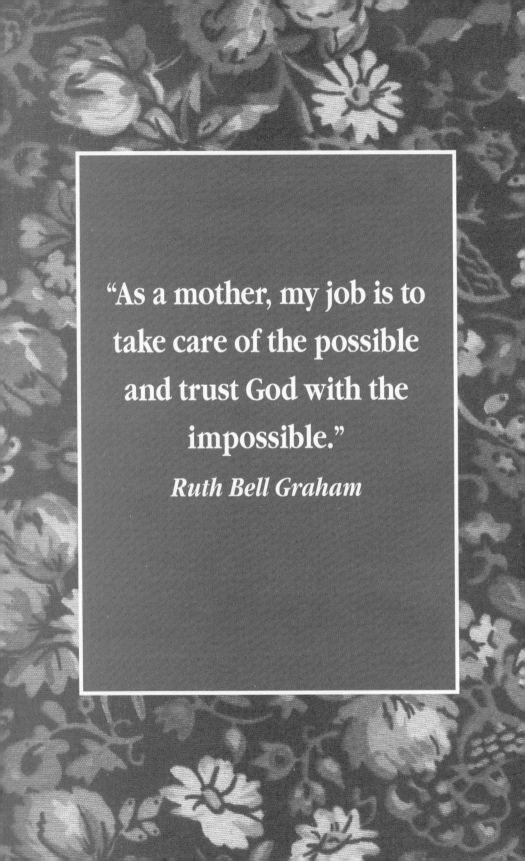

"As a mother, my job is to take care of the possible and trust God with the impossible."

Ruth Bell Graham

I

YOUR PERSONAL RELATIONSHIP
WITH GOD

THE SALVATION EXPERIENCE

*There Are Three Basic Reasons To Believe the Bible
Is the Infallible and Pure Word of God*

1. No human would have written a standard this high. Think of the best person you know. You must admit he would have left certain scriptures out had he written the Bible. So the Bible projects an inhuman standard and way of life. It has to be God because no man you know would have ever written a standard that high.

2. There is an aura, a climate, a charisma, a presence the Bible generates which no other book in the world creates. Lay an encyclopedia on your table at the restaurant, nobody will look at you twice. But when you lay your Bible on the table, they will stare at you, watch you chew your food, and even read your license plate when you get in your car! Why? The Bible creates the presence of God and forces a reaction in the hearts of men.

3. The nature of man is changed when he reads the Bible. Men change. *Peace* enters into their spirits. Joy wells up within their lives. Men like what they become when they read this book. Men accept Christ, because this Bible says Jesus Christ is the Son of God and that all have sinned and the wages of sin will bring death; and the only forgiveness that they can find is through Jesus, the Son of God.

Three Basic Reasons for Accepting Christ

1. You needed forgiveness. At some point in your life, you will want to be clean. You will hate guilt; you will crave purity. You have a built-in desire toward God, and you will have to address that appetite at some point in your life.

2. You need a friend. You may be sitting there saying, "But, don't I have friends?" Yes, but you have never had a friend like Jesus. Nobody can handle the information about your life as well as He can. He is the most consistent relationship you will ever know. Human friends vacillate in their reaction, depending on your mood or theirs. Jesus Christ never changes His opinion of you. Nobody can tell Him anything which will change His mind about you. You cannot enjoy His world without His companionship.

3. You needed a future. All men have a built-in need for immortality, a craving for an eternity. God placed it within us. D. L. Moody once made a statement, "One of these days you are going to hear that I'm dead and gone. When you do, don't believe a word of it. I'll be more alive then, than at any other time in my life." Each of us wonders about eternity. What is death like? What happens when I die? Is there a hell? a heaven? a God? a devil? What happens? Every man wants to be around tomorrow. The only guarantee you will have of a future is to have the Eternal One on the inside of you. *He is Jesus Christ, the Son of God!*

The Gospel means Good News, you can change; your sins can be forgiven; your guilt can be dissolved; God loves *you!* He wants to be the difference in your life. **All have sinned, and come short of the glory of God** (Rom. 3:23, KJV). **The wages of sin is death** (Rom. 6:23, KJV). You might say, what does that mean? It means that all unconfessed sin will be judged and penalized, but that is not the end of the story. The second part of Romans 6:23 (KJV) says, **but the gift of God is eternal life through Jesus Christ our Lord.** What does that mean? It means that between the wrath and judgment of God upon your sin, Jesus Christ the Son of God stepped in and absorbed your judgment and your penalty for you. God says if you recognize and respect Him and His worth as the Son of God, judgment will be withheld, and you will receive a pardon, forgiveness of all your mistakes.

What do you have to do? If you believe in your heart that Jesus is the Son of God and that God raised him from the dead on the third day, and confess that with your mouth, then you will be saved. (Rom. 10:9,10.) What does the word "saved" mean? *Removed from danger.* It simply means if you respect and recognize the worth of Jesus Christ, God will take you out of the danger zone and receive you as a child of the Most High God. What is His gift that you are to receive? His Son. **For God so loved the world, that he gave his only begotten Son, that whosoever believeth in him should not perish, but have everlasting life** (John 3:16, KJV). How do you accept His Son? Accept His mercy. How do you reject your sins? Confess them and turn away from them. If I confess my sins, he is faithful and just to forgive me my sins and to cleanse me from all unrighteousness. (1 John 1:9.) That is the Gospel.

≈ *Salvation Prayer* ≈

---

*H*eavenly Father, You have said in Your Word that anyone who confesses Your Son Jesus Christ as Lord and believes in his, or her, heart that You raised Him from the dead, will be saved.

I believe that Jesus is Your Son, Father, and I acknowledge that He gave His blood at Calvary to pay for my sin, sickness, poverty and spiritual death. I renounce every work of darkness, and I receive You now, Lord Jesus, as my personal Lord and Savior.

According to Your Word, Lord, I am now a new creation because I am "in Christ." My past is dead and gone, and I have new life in You. Thank You, Lord Jesus, for exchanging the unrighteousness in my life for Your righteousness. I am now the righteousness of God in You, Lord Jesus!

Scripture References:

Romans 10:9,10
2 Corinthians 5:17,21
Romans 6:23

1 Peter 2:24
Romans 3:23

➣ *How To Be Sure You Have* ➣ *Eternal Life Scriptures*

I tell you the truth, whoever hears my word and believes him who sent me has eternal life and will not be condemned; he has crossed over from death to life.

John 5:24

I tell you the truth, he who believes has everlasting life.

John 6:47

Jesus said to her, "I am the resurrection and the life. He who believes in me will live, even though he dies;

"And whoever lives and believes in me will never die. Do you believe this?"

John 11:25,26

For my Father's will is that everyone who looks to the Son and believes in him shall have eternal life, and I will raise him up at the last day.

John 6:40

My sheep listen to my voice; I know them, and they follow me.

I give them eternal life, and they shall never perish; no one can snatch them out of my hand.

John 10:27,28

The man who loves his life will lose it, while the man who hates his life in this world will keep it for eternal life.

John 12:25

For you granted him authority over all people that he might give eternal life to all those you have given him.

Now this is eternal life: that they may know you, the only true God, and Jesus Christ, whom you have sent.

John 17:2,3

For the wages of sin is death, but the gift of God is eternal life in Christ Jesus our Lord.

Romans 6:23

And this is the testimony: God has given us eternal life, and this life is in his Son.

He who has the Son has life; he who does not have the Son of God does not have life.

I write these things to you who believe in the name of the Son of God so that you may know that you have eternal life.

1 John 5:11-13

2

RECEIVING THE INFILLING
OF THE HOLY SPIRIT

**And I will pray the Father, and he shall give you another
Comforter, that he may abide with you for ever; Even the Spirit of
truth; whom the world cannot receive, because it seeth him not,
neither knoweth him: but ye know him; for he dwelleth with you,
and shall be in you.**

John 14:16,17, KJV

*O*ur Father has sent Someone to us, Someone Who will always be with us as
Comforter and Guide. He has sent the Holy Spirit.

As a Christian, you have made a choice to follow God and commit yourself to
His ways. He has given you the Holy Spirit to be with you as your direct link to
Him. But you must receive the infilling of the Holy Spirit.

The Word of God sets only two requirements for receiving the infilling of the
Holy Spirit: 1) experiencing the New Birth through Jesus Christ, and 2) asking
to receive the baptism of the Holy Spirit.

**And I say unto you, Ask, and it shall be given you; seek, and ye
shall find; knock, and it shall be opened unto you. For every one
that asketh receiveth; and he that seeketh findeth; and to him that
knocketh it shall be opened. If a son shall ask bread of any of you
that is a father, will he give him a stone? or if he ask a fish, will he
for a fish give him a serpent? Or if he shall ask an egg, will he offer**

him a scorpion? If ye then, being evil, know how to give good gifts unto your children: how much more shall your heavenly Father give the Holy Spirit to them that ask him?

Luke 11:9-13, KJV

If you have been born again as a Christian, accepting that Jesus became sin for your sins to be removed, then why should you, and how could you, cleanse yourself of any sin? You cannot cleanse yourself from sin; salvation is a free gift from God. In the same way, when you ask the Father for the Holy Spirit, He gives Him to you immediately. There is no certain manner of prayer or crying that you must perform; you just ask Him.

The Holy Spirit is a gift from the Father much like your salvation is a gift. He has given the Holy Spirit to you to draw you closer to Him for a more intimate relationship. He has also given the Holy Spirit to empower you with authority in this world.

And they were all filled with the Holy Ghost, and began to speak with other tongues, as the Spirit gave them utterance.

Acts 2:4, KJV

This clearly demonstrates what happens when you receive the infilling of the Holy Spirit with the evidence of speaking in tongues. Tongues is the Holy Spirit praying through you; not vocalizing for you, but giving you the words to speak. The language you speak is not your native language and is commonly referred to as tongues. There are wonderful benefits for praying daily in the Spirit. Praying in tongues stimulates your faith, enables you to pray for the unknown, edifies you and helps you pray in line with God's perfect will.

Realize that the Holy Spirit will give you words, but He is not going to pray for you. You will be doing the speaking with your tongue, your voice and your mouth. The Holy Spirit will bring the prompting, desire, or urge to speak. At first, it may be only a few syllables, but the more you pray, the more your language will develop.

If you do not speak in other tongues immediately, there are basically two things to check:

1) Did you sense an urging deep inside? That was the Holy Spirit prompting you. You just need to cooperate and respond by giving place to it. By faith, let the words form on your tongue.

2) If you did not sense the urging of the Holy Spirit inside you, then do not be concerned. We receive all things from God by faith, so you can educate yourself in faith by reading about the baptism of the Holy Spirit. (We recommend *Seven Vital Steps To Receiving the Holy Spirit* by Kenneth E. Hagin.) This will help you

to renew your mind and release any conscious or unconscious fear you may have had. The Bible says **faith cometh by hearing, and hearing by the word of God** (Rom. 10:17, KJV).

☜ *Infilling Prayer* ☞

---

*H*eavenly Father, I come to You in the name of Jesus to thank You because I am Your child. By faith I now receive the gift of the Holy Spirit, with the evidence of speaking in other tongues as the Holy Spirit gives me utterance.

As a Spirit-filled Christian, I am now empowered to be a victorious Christian and a bold witness of the Good News of Jesus Christ. Amen.

Scripture References:

John 14:16,17	Luke 11:13
Acts 1:8	Acts 2:4
Acts 2:38,39	Jude 20

☙ *Being Filled With the Spirit Scriptures* ☙

*B*ut you will receive power when the Holy Spirit comes on you; and you will be my witnesses in Jerusalem, and in all Judea and Samaria, and to the ends of the earth.

Acts 1:8

Do not get drunk on wine, which leads to debauchery. Instead, be filled with the Spirit.

Ephesians 5:18

The Spirit of the Lord is on me, because he has anointed me to preach good news to the poor. He has sent me to proclaim freedom for the prisoners and recovery of sight for the blind, to release the oppressed.

Luke 4:18

From the west, men will fear the name of the Lord, and from the rising of the sun, they will revere his glory. For he will come like a pent-up flood that the breath of the Lord drives along.

Isaiah 59:19

"As for me, this is my covenant with them," says the Lord. "My Spirit, who is on you, and my words that I have put in your mouth will not depart from your mouth, or from the mouths of your children, or from the mouths of their descendants from this time on and forever," says the Lord.

Isaiah 59:21

The Spirit of the Sovereign Lord is on me, because the Lord has anointed me to preach good news to the poor. He has sent me to bind up the brokenhearted, to proclaim freedom for the captives and release from darkness for the prisoners.

Isaiah 61:1

My message and my preaching were not with wise and persuasive words, but with a demonstration of the Spirit's power.

1 Corinthians 2:4

And afterward, I will pour out my Spirit on all people. Your sons and daughters will prophesy, your old men will dream dreams, your young men will see visions.

Joel 2:28

I baptize you with water for repentance. But after me will come one who is more powerful than I, whose sandals I am not fit to carry. He will baptize you with the Holy Spirit and with fire.

Matthew 3:11

I am going to send you what my Father has promised; but stay in the city until you have been clothed with power from on high.

Luke 24:49

Suddenly a sound like the blowing of a violent wind came from heaven and filled the whole house where they were sitting.

They saw what seemed to be tongues of fire that separated and came to rest on each of them.

All of them were filled with the Holy Spirit and began to speak in other tongues as the Spirit enabled them.

Peter replied, "Repent and be baptized, every one of you, in the name of Jesus Christ for the forgiveness of your sins. And you will receive the gift of the Holy Spirit."

Acts 2:2-4,38

When they arrived, they prayed for them that they might receive the Holy Spirit,

Because the Holy Spirit had not yet come upon any of them; they had simply been baptized into the name of the Lord Jesus.

Then Peter and John placed their hands on them, and they received the Holy Spirit.

Acts 8:15-17

And the disciples were filled with joy and with the Holy Spirit.

Acts 13:52

And asked them, "Did you receive the Holy Spirit when you believed?" They answered, "No, we have not even heard that there is a Holy Spirit."

So Paul asked, "Then what baptism did you receive?" "John's baptism," they replied.

Paul said, "John's baptism was a baptism of repentance. He told the people to believe in the one coming after him, that is, in Jesus."

On hearing this, they were baptized into the name of the Lord Jesus.

When Paul placed his hands on them, the Holy Spirit came on them, and they spoke in tongues and prophesied.

Acts 19:2-6

May the God of hope fill you with all joy and peace as you trust in him, so that you may overflow with hope by the power of the Holy Spirit.

Romans 15:13

3

PRINCIPLES OF BIBLE STUDY

*N*autical charts are used by sailors and maps are used by road travelers as their guidebooks and keys to their final destinations. Christians have a map and guidebook that is far superior to any other in the world – the Bible. This book is not just a great piece of literature; it is the main ingredient to a successful Christian life. The Scriptures are the inspired Word of God. Second Timothy 3:16,17 (KJV) says:

All scripture is given by inspiration of God, and is profitable for doctrine, for reproof, for correction, for instruction in righteousness: That the man of God may be perfect, throughly furnished unto all good works.

It is obvious from this passage that the Lord gave us His Word for specific reasons: to confirm our beliefs, to set spiritual and moral guidelines, to give us godly inspiration and wisdom for our daily living, and to instruct us in the ways of our Father. We cannot draw these things from the Word of God without daily study.

There are many ways to study the Bible, each with its own merit. Here are a few principles that will help you study earnestly.

1. Always have the right attitude toward studying your Bible. Approach your daily study with an open heart and mind. Be ready to accept what the Lord has to show you.

2. Realize that studying your Bible isn't always easy. Sometimes reading and studying are hard work. Make yourself be consistent and faithful to daily study, and be a diligent student of God's Word. A systematic approach to Bible study can help you overcome difficult periods in your study times.

3. Keep a record of what you have learned. Write down what the Lord reveals to you during your study times. This will help you put your new wisdom to practice and provide a permanent record for you to refer to when you need it.

4. Share with others what you have learned. Often, if you are willing, the Lord will show you a key to a problem that someone else can use, too. His wisdom is too wonderful to be kept hidden. Encourage someone else by sharing with him how your study time has strengthened you.

5. Your study time is meant to add to worship and teaching services, not replace them. This is your private, personal time for you to learn what your Father has in store for you, but it is meant to augment your fellowship at church and other meetings with believers. Your personal study time is not meant to be your own source of fellowship with the Lord.

6. Find a consistent time and place to study. For example, you might start with ten to fifteen minutes a day with an eventual goal of thirty minutes. Many people prefer to study in the mornings so that they can be receptive to God and His wisdom throughout the day. The key is to find what works for you.

7. Be in an attitude of prayer while you read. Ask the Holy Spirit to be your guide through the Scriptures. The Holy Spirit was given to help you grow in relationship with the Father, and that includes Bible study!

∼ *Prayer To Walk in the Word* ∼

Father, in the name of Jesus, I accept Your Word as my road map for a successful life. I accept Your Word as the stabilizing force in my life, for You said it is forever settled in heaven.

Thank You, Father, that You have personalized Your Word for me. Because it is my standard for integrity, my guide for spiritual and moral principles and my daily inspiration and source of wisdom, I will meditate upon Your Word day and night.

I will give Your Word first place in my life, Father, for to walk in Your Word is to walk in relationship and in fellowship with You, with Jesus Christ Your Son and with the Holy Spirit. To walk in Your Word is to walk in victory in this life.

Because I want to know You more, Lord, I will delight myself in Your Word continually. Amen.

Scripture References:

Psalm 119:89　　　　　　　　　Joshua 1:8

Mark 13:31　　　　　　　　　　Psalm 119:105

Psalm 1:2

∝ *Studying God's Word Scriptures* ∝

*D*o not let this Book of the Law depart from your mouth; meditate on it day and night, so that you may be careful to do everything written in it. Then you will be prosperous and successful.

Joshua 1:8

All Scripture is God-breathed and is useful for teaching, rebuking, correcting and training in righteousness.

2 Timothy 3:16

Heaven and earth will pass away, but my words will never pass away.

Mark 13:31

Jesus answered, "It is written: 'Man does not live on bread alone, but on every word that comes from the mouth of God.'"

Matthew 4:4

For the word of God is living and active. Sharper than any double-edged sword, it penetrates even to dividing soul and spirit, joints and marrow; it judges the thoughts and attitudes of the heart.

Hebrews 4:12

For prophecy never had its origin in the will of man, but men spoke from God as they were carried along by the Holy Spirit.

2 Peter 1:21

But his delight is in the law of the Lord, and on his law he meditates day and night.

Psalm 1:2

Your word is a lamp to my feet and a light for my path.

Psalm 119:105

In God, whose word I praise, in God I trust; I will not be afraid. What can mortal man do to me?

Psalm 56:4

For everything that was written in the past was written to teach us, so that through endurance and the encouragement of the Scriptures we might have hope.

Romans 15:4

The grass withers and the flowers fall, but the word of our God stands forever.

Isaiah 40:8

He sent forth his word and healed them; he rescued them from the grave.

Psalm 107:20

Like newborn babies, crave pure spiritual milk, so that by it you may grow up in your salvation.

1 Peter 2:2

Do not merely listen to the word, and so deceive yourselves. Do what it says.

James 1:22

To the Jews who had believed him, Jesus said, "If you hold to my teaching, you are really my disciples.
"Then you will know the truth, and the truth will set you free."

John 8:31,32

Consequently, faith comes from hearing the message, and the message is heard through the word of Christ.

Romans 10:17

But the word of the Lord stands forever. And this is the word that was preached to you.

1 Peter 1:25

He remembers his covenant forever, the word he commanded, for a thousand generations.

1 Chronicles 16:15

So is my word that goes out from my mouth: It will not return to me empty, but will accomplish what I desire and achieve the purpose for which I sent it.

Isaiah 55:11

④

"IN-CHRIST" REALITIES

*I*n Revelation 12:11, the Word says the saints overcame the accuser by the blood of Jesus and the *word of their testimony*. That is true not only for end-time martyrs, but it is true for born-again children of God living everyday lives in any generation.

However, you cannot have a "testimony" unless you know the "rights" of a born-again child of God, the things you inherited in, through, and with Jesus because of His work on the cross.

You must know who you are *in Christ*. Then, to bring those things *that you already possess* into manifestation, you must begin to believe them. To be born again, you must have faith that God exists and that He sent His only begotten Son to die for your sins because He loves you. (John 3:16.) Salvation is a free gift for you, purchased by Jesus, but unless you believe that and *confess* it with your mouth, salvation is not manifested in you. It is not a reality for you. (Rom. 10:9,10.)

First, find out from the Word what things are already yours because of Jesus. Then, if you want to build faith for those things to become real in your life, begin to speak out the good things God has done and the things you are believing for Him to do.

Faith without works is dead. (James 2:17.) Faith grows stronger by telling testimonies of Jesus, by continual confession of what you believe God will do.

A weak confession is one full of doubt and is a confession of defeat. As long as people talk defeat, they will not overcome. They have the blood of the Lamb, but the true "word of their testimony" is missing.

What *is* the confession, the word of our testimony, that we are told in Hebrews 4:14 to "hold fast"? It is the positive things God has done *in* our lives and *for* us. The word of our testimony is speaking out of who we are *in Christ*, not just what He has done for us in our natural lives.

From God's viewpoint, everything His Word says you are, or that you have, is true. Those things already are done! The Bible is a legal document setting forth the story, the description, and the provisions of the Blood Covenant, of which the Abrahamic Covenant (the Old Covenant) was a forerunner.

There are more than one hundred expressions such as "in Christ," "in Him," "in Whom," "through Whom," and so forth in the New Testament that set forth all the things Jesus provided for us by His blood on the cross of Calvary.

Start with Second Corinthians 5:17 (KJV):

Therefore if any man be *in Christ*, he is a new creature: old things are passed away; behold, all things are become new.

Then go on and memorize as many others as you can, confessing them often, so that the "word of your testimony" is in line with the Word of God. Finding out the reality of who you are *in Christ* will change your life!

～ *Prayer to Be God-Inside Minded* ～

---

*F*ather, You created me a three-part being: spirit, soul and body. My spirit, soul and body are nurtured daily with Your Word. Your Word strengthens my spirit, renews my mind, and brings control to my body, which is a temple of Your Spirit. I submit every area of my life to Your Word, Lord. You and Your Word are one.

Thank You, Holy Spirit, that You dominate my human spirit. I am led and controlled by Your Spirit in the daily affairs of life, Lord, rather than by my flesh.

I think good thoughts because Your Spirit dominates my mind, Lord, and my thoughts create in me a picture of who I am in You.

I am quick to obey Your voice, which causes me to triumph in every circumstance I face.

Scripture References:

1 Thessalonians 5:23	Romans 8:14,16
1 Corinthians 6:19,20	2 Corinthians 2:14
Proverbs 23:7	

❧ *Knowing Who You Are in Christ Scriptures* ❧

*N*o, in all these things we are more than conquerors through him who loved us.

Romans 8:37

For everyone born of God overcomes the world. This is the victory that has overcome the world, even our faith.

1 John 5:4

But thanks be to God, who always leads us in triumphal procession in Christ and through us spreads everywhere the fragrance of the knowledge of him.

2 Corinthians 2:14

But thanks be to God! He gives us the victory through our Lord Jesus Christ.

1 Corinthians 15:57

I can do everything through him who gives me strength.

Philippians 4:13

What, then, shall we say in response to this? If God is for us, who can be against us?

Romans 8:31

He replied, "Because you have so little faith. I tell you the truth, if you have faith as small as a mustard seed, you can say to this mountain, 'Move from here to there' and it will move. Nothing will be impossible for you."

Matthew 17:20

Jesus looked at them and said, "With man this is impossible, but with God all things are possible."

Matthew 19:26

For we are God's workmanship, created in Christ Jesus to do good works, which God prepared in advance for us to do.

Ephesians 2:10

I have been crucified with Christ and I no longer live, but Christ lives in me. The life I live in the body, I live by faith in the Son of God, who loved me and gave himself for me.

Galatians 2:20

Jesus looked at them and said, "With man this is impossible, but not with God; all things are possible with God."

Mark 10:27

For nothing is impossible with God.

Luke 1:37

Jesus replied, "What is impossible with men is possible with God."

Luke 18:27

Therefore, if anyone is in Christ, he is a new creation; the old has gone, the new has come!

2 Corinthians 5:17

God made him who had no sin to be sin for us, so that in him we might become the righteousness of God.

2 Corinthians 5:21

How great is the love the Father has lavished on us, that we should be called children of God! And that is what we are! The reason the world does not know us is that it did not know him.

Dear friends, now we are children of God, and what we will be has not yet been made known. But we know that when he appears, we shall be like him, for we shall see him as he is.

1 John 3:1,2

The Spirit himself testifies with our spirit that we are God's children. Now if we are children, then we are heirs – heirs of God and co-heirs with Christ, if indeed we share in his sufferings in order that we may also share in his glory.

Romans 8:16,17

"For in him we live and move and have our being." As some of your own poets have said, "We are his offspring."

Acts 17:28

And God raised us up with Christ and seated us with him in the heavenly realms in Christ Jesus.

Ephesians 2:6

OTHER SCRIPTURES TO HELP YOU LIVE THE VICTORIOUS CHRISTIAN LIFE

 Developing Your Prayer Life

*I*f you believe, you will receive whatever you ask for in prayer.

Matthew 21:22

Do not be anxious about anything, but in everything, by prayer and petition, with thanksgiving, present your requests to God.

Philippians 4:6

And the prayer offered in faith will make the sick person well; the Lord will raise him up. If he has sinned, he will be forgiven.

James 5:15

If my people, who are called by my name, will humble themselves and pray and seek my face and turn from their wicked ways, then will I hear from heaven and will forgive their sin and will heal their land.

2 Chronicles 7:14

Ask and it will be given to you; seek and you will find; knock and the door will be opened to you.

For everyone who asks receives; he who seeks finds; and to him who knocks, the door will be opened.

Matthew 7:7,8

I tell you the truth, if anyone says to this mountain, "Go, throw yourself into the sea," and does not doubt in his heart but believes that what he says will happen, it will be done for him.

Therefore I tell you, whatever you ask for in prayer, believe that you have received it, and it will be yours.

Mark 11:23,24

If you remain in me and my words remain in you, ask whatever you wish, and it will be given you.

John 15:7

Again, I tell you that if two of you on earth agree about anything you ask for, it will be done for you by my Father in heaven.

Matthew 18:19

And I will do whatever you ask in my name, so that the Son may bring glory to the Father.

You may ask me for anything in my name, and I will do it.

John 14:13,14

In that day you will no longer ask me anything. I tell you the truth, my Father will give you whatever you ask in my name.

Until now you have not asked for anything in my name. Ask and you will receive, and your joy will be complete.

John 16:23,24

But you, dear friends, build yourselves up in your most holy faith and pray in the Holy Spirit.

Jude 20

This is the confidence we have in approaching God: that if we ask anything according to his will, he hears us.

And if we know that he hears us – whatever we ask – we know that we have what we asked of him.

1 John 5:14,15

Let us then approach the throne of grace with confidence, so that we may receive mercy and find grace to help us in our time of need.

Hebrews 4:16

Therefore confess your sins to each other and pray for each other so that you may be healed. The prayer of a righteous man is powerful and effective.

James 5:16

The eyes of the Lord are on the righteous and his ears are attentive to their cry.

Psalm 34:15

Before they call I will answer; while they are still speaking I will hear.

Isaiah 65:24

Call to me and I will answer you and tell you great and unsearchable things you do not know.

Jeremiah 33:3

If you believe, you will receive whatever you ask for in prayer.

Matthew 21:22

I keep asking that the God of our Lord Jesus Christ, the glorious Father, may give you the Spirit of wisdom and revelation, so that you may know him better.

I pray also that the eyes of your heart may be enlightened in order that you may know the hope to which he has called you, the riches of his glorious inheritance in the saints,

And his incomparably great power for us who believe. That power is like the working of his mighty strength,

Which he exerted in Christ when he raised him from the dead and seated him at his right hand in the heavenly realms,

Far above all rule and authority, power and dominion, and every title that can be given, not only in the present age but also in the one to come.

And God placed all things under his feet and appointed him to be head over everything for the church,

Which is his body, the fullness of him who fills everything in every way.

Ephesians 1:17-23

For this reason I kneel before the Father,

From whom his whole family in heaven and on earth derives its name.

I pray that out of his glorious riches he may strengthen you with power through his Spirit in your inner being,

So that Christ may dwell in your hearts through faith. And I pray that you, being rooted and established in love,

May have power, together with all the saints, to grasp how wide and long and high and deep is the love of Christ,

And to know this love that surpasses knowledge – that you may be filled to the measure of all the fullness of God.

Now to him who is able to do immeasurably more than all we ask or imagine, according to his power that is at work within us,

To him be glory in the church and in Christ Jesus throughout all generations, for ever and ever! Amen.

Ephesians 3:14-21

And pray in the Spirit on all occasions with all kinds of prayers and requests. With this in mind, be alert and always keep on praying for all the saints.

Pray also for me, that whenever I open my mouth, words may be given me so that I will fearlessly make known the mystery of the gospel,

For which I am an ambassador in chains. Pray that I may declare it fearlessly, as I should.

Ephesians 6:18-20

For this reason, since the day we heard about you, we have not stopped praying for you and asking God to fill you with the knowledge of his will through all spiritual wisdom and understanding.

And we pray this in order that you may live a life worthy of the Lord and may please him in every way: bearing fruit in every good work, growing in the knowledge of God,

Being strengthened with all power according to his glorious might so that you may have great endurance and patience, and joyfully

Giving thanks to the Father, who has qualified you to share in the inheritance of the saints in the kingdom of light.

For he has rescued us from the dominion of darkness and brought us into the kingdom of the Son he loves,

In whom we have redemption, the forgiveness of sins.

Colossians 1:9-14

≈ *Praising and Worshipping God* ≈

They were also to stand every morning to thank and praise the Lord. They were to do the same in the evening.

1 Chronicles 23:30

The Lord is my strength and my shield; my heart trusts in him, and I am helped. My heart leaps for joy and I will give thanks to him in song.

Psalm 28:7

I will extol the Lord at all times; his praise will always be on my lips.

Psalm 34:1

Then we your people, the sheep of your pasture, will praise you forever; from generation to generation we will recount your praise.

Psalm 79:13

It is good to praise the Lord and make music to your name, O Most High, To proclaim your love in the morning and your faithfulness at night.

Psalm 92:1,2

O Lord, you are my God; I will exalt you and praise your name, for in perfect faithfulness you have done marvelous things, things planned long ago.

Isaiah 25:1

I will praise the Lord all my life; I will sing praise to my God as long as I live.

Psalm 146:2

Ascribe to the Lord the glory due his name; worship the Lord in the splendor of his holiness.

Psalm 29:2

Come, let us bow down in worship, let us kneel before the Lord our Maker.

Psalm 95:6

Yet a time is coming and has now come when the true worshipers will worship the Father in spirit and truth, for they are the kind of worshipers the Father seeks.

God is spirit, and his worshipers must worship in spirit and in truth.

John 4:23,24

I praise you because I am fearfully and wonderfully made; your works are wonderful, I know that full well.

Psalm 139:14

From birth I have relied on you; you brought me forth from my mother's womb. I will ever praise you.

Psalm 71:6

My tongue will speak of your righteousness and of your praises all day long.

Psalm 35:28

≈ *Obedience* ≈

---

*I*f you are willing and obedient, you will eat the best from the land.

Isaiah 1:19

All the ways of the Lord are loving and faithful for those who keep the demands of his covenant.

Psalm 25:10

The fear of the Lord is the beginning of wisdom; all who follow his precepts have good understanding. To him belongs eternal praise.

Psalm 111:10

Teach me to do your will, for you are my God; may your good Spirit lead me on level ground.

Psalm 143:10

For whoever does the will of my Father in heaven is my brother and sister and mother.

Matthew 12:50

Peter and the other apostles replied: "We must obey God rather than men!"

Acts 5:29

This is how we know that we love the children of God: by loving God and carrying out his commands.
This is the love for God: to obey his commands. And his commands are not burdensome.

1 John 5:2,3

And the people said to Joshua, "We will serve the Lord our God and obey him."

Joshua 24:24

Now if you obey me fully and keep my covenant, then out of all nations you will be my treasured possession.

Exodus 19:5a

If you love me, you will obey what I command.

John 14:15

❧ *Understanding Your Authority Over the Devil* ❧

*A*nd these signs will accompany those who believe: In my name they will drive out demons; they will speak in new tongues.

Mark 16:17

And do not give the devil a foothold.

Ephesians 4:27

Finally, be strong in the Lord and in his mighty power.

Put on the full armor of God so that you can take your stand against the devil's schemes.

For our struggle is not against flesh and blood, but against the rulers, against the authorities, against the powers of this dark world and against the spiritual forces of evil in the heavenly realms.

Therefore put on the full armor of God, so that when the day of evil comes, you may be able to stand your ground, and after you have done everything, to stand.

Stand firm then, with the belt of truth buckled around your waist, with the breastplate of righteousness in place,

And with your feet fitted with the readiness that comes from the gospel of peace.

In addition to all this, take up the shield of faith, with which you can extinguish all the flaming arrows of the evil one.

Take the helmet of salvation and the sword of the Spirit, which is the word of God.

And pray in the Spirit on all occasions with all kinds of prayers and requests. With this in mind, be alert and always keep on praying for all the saints.

Ephesians 6:10-18

For though we live in the world, we do not wage war as the world does.

The weapons we fight with are not the weapons of the world. On the contrary, they have divine power to demolish strongholds.

We demolish arguments and every pretension that sets itself up against the knowledge of God, and we take captive every thought to make it obedient to Christ.

2 Corinthians 10:3-5

The Lord will rescue me from every evil attack and will bring me safely to his heavenly kingdom. To him be glory for ever and ever. Amen.

2 Timothy 4:18

If this is so, then the Lord knows how to rescue godly men from trials and to hold the unrighteous for the day of judgment, while continuing their punishment.

2 Peter 2:9

Be self-controlled and alert. Your enemy the devil prowls around like a roaring lion looking for someone to devour.

1 Peter 5:8

Submit yourselves, then, to God. Resist the devil, and he will flee from you.

James 4:7

How God anointed Jesus of Nazareth with the Holy Spirit and power, and how he went around doing good and healing all who were under the power of the devil, because God was with him.

Acts 10:38

When Jesus had called the Twelve together, he gave them power and authority to drive out all demons and to cure diseases.

Luke 9:1

I have given you authority to trample on snakes and scorpions and to overcome all the power of the enemy; nothing will harm you.

Luke 10:19

As for you, you were dead in your transgressions and sins,
In which you used to live when you followed the ways of this world and of the ruler of the kingdom of the air, the spirit who is now at work in those who are disobedient.

All of us also lived among them at one time, gratifying the cravings of our sinful nature and following its desires and thoughts. Like the rest, we were by nature objects of wrath.

But because of his great love for us, God, who is rich in mercy,

Made us alive with Christ even when we were dead in transgressions – it is by grace you have been saved.

And God raised us up with Christ and seated us with him in the heavenly realms in Christ Jesus.

Ephesians 2:1-6

"A virtuous woman trusts Jesus completely because she knows Him. And she knows Him because she has spent time with Him. As a believer, the potential for excellence is within us. God has given us the key, the Bible, to unlock our treasure chest and expose His glorious nature to those around us. The question is not 'Does the Proverbs 31 woman exist within you?' But 'Who can find her?' You can."

Janice Subers

II. A VIRTUOUS WOMAN

6

A VIRTUOUS WOMAN

Who can find a virtuous woman? for her price is far above rubies. The heart of her husband doth safely trust in her, so that he shall have no need of spoil.

She will do him good and not evil all the days of her life.

She seeketh wool, and flax, and worketh willingly with her hands.

She is like the merchants' ships; she bringeth her food from afar.

She riseth also while it is yet night, and giveth meat to her household, and a portion to her maidens.

She considereth a field, and buyeth it: with the fruit of her hands she planteth a vineyard.

She girdeth her loins with strength, and strengtheneth her arms.

She perceiveth that her merchandise is good: her candle goeth not out by night.

She layeth her hands to the spindle, and her hands hold the distaff.

She stretcheth out her hand to the poor; yea, she reacheth forth her hands to the needy.

She is not afraid of the snow for her household: for all her household are clothed with scarlet.

She maketh herself coverings of tapestry; her clothing is silk and purple.

Her husband is known in the gates, when he sitteth among the elders of the land.

She maketh fine linen, and selleth it; and delivereth girdles unto the merchant.

Strength and honour are her clothing; and she shall rejoice in time to come.

She openeth her mouth with wisdom; and in her tongue is the law of kindness.

She looketh well to the ways of her household, and eateth not the bread of idleness.

Her children arise up, and call her blessed; her husband also, and he praiseth her.

Many daughters have done virtuously, but thou excellest them all.

Favour is deceitful, and beauty is vain: but a woman that feareth the Lord, she shall be praised.

Give her of the fruit of her hands; and let her own works praise her in the gates.

Proverbs 31:10-31, KJV

"A BIBLE LOOK AT WOMAN, WIFE, AND MOTHER"

BY PAT HARRISON

*E*very woman, whether single, married, or divorced, can profit from a study of what the Word of God has to say on the subject of woman, wife, and mother. If single now, perhaps you will be involved as a wife and mother someday. If not, you can still minister to others by gaining knowledge on this topic. There is always counseling to be done; and when you get women to realize how beautiful it is that God created them women, that settles many problems. Those whose children are gone from home can learn things that will minister life to their grandchildren.

The second chapter of Genesis gives us insight into the creation of woman. I believe that by studying this portion of Scripture, women will be thrilled when they see that God saw fit to create them women.

Let's begin with Genesis 2:7:

Then the Lord God formed man from the dust of the ground and breathed into his nostrils the breath or spirit of life, and man became a living being.

And the Lord God planted a garden toward the east, in Eden [delight]; and there He put the man whom He had formed (framed, constituted).

And out of the ground the Lord God made to grow every tree that is pleasant to the sight or to be desired — good (suitable, pleasant) for food; the tree of life also in the center of the garden, and the tree of knowledge of [the difference between] good and evil and blessing and calamity.

Genesis 2:7-9, AMP

Now let's skip to the fifteenth verse:

And the Lord God took the man and put him in the Garden of Eden to tend and guard and keep it.

And the Lord God commanded the man, saying, You may freely eat of every tree of the garden;

But of the tree of the knowledge of good and evil and blessing and calamity you shall not eat, for in the day that you eat of it you shall surely die.

Now the Lord God said, It is not good (sufficient, satisfactory) that the man should be alone; I will make him a helper meet (suitable, adapted, complementary) for him.

Genesis 2:15-18, AMP

The Scripture goes on to tell how God formed the animals and beasts and let Adam name them. But God still saw that for Adam there was not a helper who was adaptable, suitable, and completing for him. So in Genesis 2:21-25 (AMP) we are told:

And the Lord God caused a deep sleep to fall upon Adam; and while he slept, He took one of his ribs or a part of his side and closed up the [place with] flesh.

And the rib or part of his side which the Lord God had taken from the man He built up and made into a woman, and He brought her to the man.

Then Adam said, This [creature] is now bone of my bones and flesh of my flesh; she shall be called Woman, because she was taken out of a man.

Therefore a man shall leave his father and his mother and shall become united and cleave to his wife, and they shall become one flesh.

And the man and his wife were both naked and were not embarrassed or ashamed in each other's presence.

I want to lay a foundation here, so you can see some differences between man and woman. Genesis 2:7 tells us God formed man. In the original Hebrew, one definition of being formed is "squeezed together." That is why man, many times, appears rugged.

But in verse 22, where we are told about God creating woman, the Hebrew means "skillfully and carefully handcrafted."

The Lord showed me that this was so a woman would be desired and admired.

God says this woman was to be a "helper meet." The word *help* means "to give aid and assistance," and the word *meet* means "to surround." You could say the woman is to continually surround with aid and assistance.

That is what you are as a helper meet. You are skillfully and carefully handcrafted to be suitable, adaptable, and completing to a man. The way you become those things is by continually surrounding the one God has given you with aid and assistance.

Once you've accepted yourself as a woman, you are proud because your Creator saw fit to create you. He saw that you could flow and walk in that to perfection. God sees every creation as good and perfect – and that's how you're to see yourself! When you see yourself that way, you will see your mate that way. That's important. You weren't made for man to see himself differently than how God made him, but you were created to make yourself adaptable, suitable, and completing for him.

We read in Genesis 2:24 (AMP), **Therefore a man shall leave his father and his mother and shall become united and cleave to his wife, and they shall become one flesh.**

The word *cleave* in the Hebrew means "to never stop chasing." If you, as the woman, continually surround your husband with aid and assistance, he will never stop chasing you! You are making him complete at all times; therefore, he desires to be around you. He always desires to have you with him so he is complete.

The Church has a relationship with Jesus which parallels that between husband and wife. We are the Church, the Bride, and He is the Bridegroom. When we look to Him, and go forth doing what we are placed on this earth to do, then He meets our every need. But when we're not going forth, being His arms extended, there is that sense of not feeling Him around us – not being aware He is there.

When you, as a woman (because you were created for man), do not function as you should, making yourself suitable, adaptable, and completing for your husband, you don't have the sense of fulfillment that is needed for him. That's because you're not doing what you're supposed to be doing.

You have a big responsibility. It is important that you function as God created you. Woman was created perfect – not just for God, but for man. That was lost in the Garden when Adam sold out to Satan, but through Jesus it has been restored. And through that restoration, through spiritual adoption in Jesus Christ, we can again be the perfect woman God created us to be. We are that unto God and man.

The Bible tells us that God placed the Tree of Life in the middle of the Garden. It was the Tree of Life which kept Adam and Eve perfect. Today we can see the parallel in Jesus. He is the tree of life to us. By always feeding upon Jesus, the Word, we dwell and continue in our perfection in Him. We know who we are in Christ, and we can be just as He expects us to be. We can do just as He expects us to do. He is the One Who brought back the perfection that was lost in the Garden.

The Word tells us that when we accept Jesus we are a new creation. Our spirit, the real us, is perfect. This spirit within us makes us function and be perfected as we should here on this earth. We have to realize that, and walk in it. It's important to meditate on the Word in these areas.

Sometimes we have difficulty with a certain thing. We think, "Why is this becoming so hard for me?" Then we realize we've not been meditating in the Word as we should. It's not that we've lost the Word, but we've lost our awareness of it. We haven't been speaking it out. When we hear the Word, it penetrates within and becomes a reality. When it's spoken out, the manifestation is complete. The Word has to be a part of us, but that will not happen until we feed on it continually.

We cannot receive strength and nourishment from food by simply sitting and looking at it every day at mealtime. But people will look at the Word and think, *I don't know what that means.* They'll put it on the shelf. It would be the same way in the natural if we sat down at the table and said, "I can't tell if that food would do me any good."

The Word is not just paper and ink – it's life. And we need to be established through the Word on this subject of woman, wife, and mother.

Let's look at a New Testament scripture that shows again how woman was created for man.

Neither was man created on account of or for the benefit of woman, but woman on account of and for the benefit of man.
Therefore she should [be subject to his authority and should] have a covering on her head [as a token, a symbol, of her

submission to authority, that she may show reverence as do] the angels [and not displease them].

Nevertheless, in [the plan of] the Lord and from His point of view woman is not apart from and independent of man, nor is man aloof from and independent of woman;

For as woman was made from man, even so man is also born of woman, and all [whether male or female go forth] from God [as their Author].

1 Corinthians 11:9-12, AMP

We see again why God created woman. First Corinthians 11:7 tells us man is the image and reflected glory of God, and that woman is the expression of man's glory, his majesty, and preeminence. That's the reason we should respect the position he is in and honor him. In doing that, we cause him to be complete and to function on this earth as God intended.

That's part of our adapting and being suitable – part of our responsibility as a woman. The husband/wife relationship is not just something the world thought up. It's from God.

It is so important that before you marry you establish your relationship with the Father God. If you know Him intimately, then the natural laws which cause you to be effective to a man automatically fall into place. You have such a relationship and fellowship with God that you know how He created you and why, and you can flow in that. You know what you are supposed to do.

The Bible says we are to submit ourselves to our husbands. Submission is an attitude of the heart – not a physical action. That's why the Bible says to submit to your husband as to the Lord. (Eph. 5:22.) How do you submit yourself to Jesus? With an attitude of love.

In a marriage, you understand authority, you understand your husband's position, you understand submission – and you have no problem submitting.

You are not going to be a robot – but you and your husband will form a union. That is what God desires. Because you were made for man, you have a responsibility to look at marriage this way.

If we are submitted to Jesus and He is Lord of our life, we should not wonder what He can do for us, but we should ask, "What can we do for Him?" We can reach out and bring other people into balance by bringing them to Him, being ministers of reconciliation. We bring balance, too – and completion – to the marriage union.

Since we were also made for man, we need to see what we can do for him. That way, by adapting ourselves, and by making ourselves suitable and completing, we will reap the benefits of the law of giving and receiving.

Love never fails. And you do this through love. Your husband has to respond to love, because love draws – it never pushes away.

If in your marriage there are times you feel you're being separated or drawn away from your husband, don't get your eyes on the circumstances or your mate (saying he does this or that). Check up on yourself. The Lord can show you areas where you are not fulfilling your role as you should. When you begin to adapt, everything will come into perspective.

As woman, because we have been classified as the weaker sex, we want to sit down and let man wait on us, put us up on a pedestal because we're delicate, and do things that are supposed to be done for a lady. But that isn't the way it is.

Man and woman are equal in the sight of God. He created you for man; you're strong. You are perfect in the Lord Jesus Christ.

So be suitable, adaptable, and completing to your husband, continually surrounding him with aid and assistance. In that way, you will be following the role of woman that God created you for. You will be the joy your husband desires, and yes, you will be the only person in his life. And He will lift you up.

WHEN YOU WANT TO BE...
SCRIPTURES

 A Patient Mother

$\mathcal{B}$e still before the Lord and wait patiently for him; do not fret when men succeed in their ways, when they carry out their wicked schemes.

Psalm 37:7

I waited patiently for the Lord; he turned to me and heard my cry.

Psalm 40:1

For you have been my hope, O Sovereign Lord, my confidence since my youth.

Psalm 71:5

The end of a matter is better than its beginning, and patience is better than pride.

Do not be quickly provoked in your spirit, for anger resides in the lap of fools.

Ecclesiastes 7:8,9

But those who hope in the Lord will renew their strength. They will soar on wings like eagles; they will run and not grow weary, they will walk and not be faint.

Isaiah 40:31

But blessed is the man who trusts in the Lord, whose confidence is in him.

Jeremiah 17:7

By standing firm you will gain life.

Luke 21:19

Not only so, but we also rejoice in our sufferings, because we know that suffering produces perseverance; perseverance, character; and character, hope.

And hope does not disappoint us, because God has poured out his love into our hearts by the Holy Spirit, whom he has given us.

Romans 5:3-5

But if we hope for what we do not yet have, we wait for it patiently.

Romans 8:25

For everything that was written in the past was written to teach us, so that through endurance and the encouragement of the Scriptures we might have hope.

May the God who gives endurance and encouragement give you a spirit of unity among yourselves as you follow Christ Jesus.

May the God of hope fill you with all joy and peace as you trust in him, so that you may overflow with hope by the power of the Holy Spirit.

Romans 15:4,5,13

But the fruit of the Spirit is love, joy, peace, patience, kindness, goodness, faithfulness.

Galatians 5:22

I can do everything through him who gives me strength.

Philippians 4:13

We do not want you to become lazy, but to imitate those who through faith and patience inherit what has been promised.

Hebrews 6:12

So do not throw away your confidence; it will be richly rewarded.

You need to persevere so that when you have done the will of God, you will receive what he has promised.

For in just a very little while, "He who is coming will come and will not delay."

Hebrews 10:35-37

Because you know that the testing of your faith develops perseverance.
Perseverance must finish its work so that you may be mature and complete, not lacking anything.

James 1:3,4

Be patient, then, brothers, until the Lord's coming. See how the farmer waits for the land to yield its valuable crop and how patient he is for the autumn and spring rains.
You too, be patient and stand firm, because the Lord's coming is near.

James 5:7,8

For this very reason, make every effort to add to your faith goodness; and to goodness, knowledge; and to knowledge, self-control; and to self-control, perseverance; and to perseverance, godliness.

2 Peter 1:5,6

☞ *A Loving Mother* ☞

---

*H*atred stirs up dissension, but love covers over all wrongs.

Proverbs 10:12

Many waters cannot quench love; rivers cannot wash it away. If one were to give all the wealth of his house for love, it would be utterly scorned.

Song of Solomon 8:7

A new command I give you: Love one another. As I have loved you, so you must love one another.
By this all men will know that you are my disciples, if you love one another.

John 13:34,35

As the Father has loved me, so have I loved you. Now remain in my love.
If you obey my commands, you will remain in my love, just as I have obeyed my Father's commands and remain in his love.
My command is this: Love each other as I have loved you.

Greater love has no one than this, that he lay down his life for his friends. You are my friends if you do what I command.

I no longer call you servants, because a servant does not know his master's business. Instead, I have called you friends, for everything that I learned from my Father I have made known to you.

You did not choose me, but I chose you and appointed you to go and bear fruit – fruit that will last. Then the Father will give you whatever you ask in my name.

This is my command: Love each other.

John 15:9,10,12-17

Let no debt remain outstanding, except the continuing debt to love one another, for he who loves his fellowman has fulfilled the law.

Love does no harm to its neighbor. Therefore love is the fulfillment of the law.

Romans 13:8,10

If I speak in the tongues of men and of angels, but have not love, I am only a resounding gong or a clanging cymbal.

If I have the gift of prophecy and can fathom all mysteries and all knowledge, and if I have a faith that can move mountains, but have not love, I am nothing.

If I give all I possess to the poor and surrender my body to the flames, but have not love, I gain nothing.

Love is patient, love is kind. It does not envy, it does not boast, it is not proud.

It is not rude, it is not self-seeking, it is not easily angered, it keeps no record of wrongs.

Love does not delight in evil but rejoices with the truth.

It always protects, always trusts, always hopes, always perseveres.

Love never fails.

1 Corinthians 13:1-8a

And now these three remain: faith, hope and love. But the greatest of these is love.

1 Corinthians 13:13

And live a life of love, just as Christ loved us and gave himself up for us as a fragrant offering and sacrifice to God.

Ephesians 5:2

May the Lord make your love increase and overflow for each other and for everyone else, just as ours does for you.

1 Thessalonians 3:12

God is not unjust; he will not forget your work and the love you have shown him as you have helped his people and continue to help them.

Hebrews 6:10

And let us consider how we may spur one another on toward love and good deeds.

Hebrews 10:24

If you really keep the royal law found in Scripture, "Love your neighbor as yourself," you are doing right.

James 2:8

This is the message you heard from the beginning: We should love one another.

1 John 3:11

We know that we have passed from death to life, because we love our brothers. Anyone who does not love remains in death.

1 John 3:14

Dear children, let us not love with words or tongue but with actions and in truth.

1 John 3:18

Dear friends, let us love one another, for love comes from God. Everyone who loves has been born of God and knows God.

Whoever does not love does not know God, because God is love.

1 John 4:7,8

Above all, love each other deeply, because love covers over a multitude of sins.

1 Peter 4:8

≫ *A Giving Mother* ≪

*B*ring the whole tithe into the storehouse, that there may be food in my house. Test me in this," says the Lord Almighty, "and see if I will not throw open the floodgates of heaven and pour out so much blessing that you will not have room enough for it.

"I will prevent pests from devouring your crops, and the vines in your fields will not cast their fruit," says the Lord Almighty.

"Then all the nations will call you blessed, for yours will be a delightful land," says the Lord Almighty.

Malachi 3:10-12

But as for you, be strong and do not give up, for your work will be rewarded.

2 Chronicles 15:7

Good will come to him who is generous and lends freely, who conducts his affairs with justice.

Psalm 112:5

Honor the Lord with your wealth, with the firstfruits of all your crops; then your barns will be filled to overflowing, and your vats will brim over with new wine.

Proverbs 3:9,10

He who is kind to the poor lends to the Lord, and he will reward him for what he has done.

Proverbs 19:17

A generous man will himself be blessed, for he shares his food with the poor.

Proverbs 22:9

He who gives to the poor will lack nothing, but he who closes his eyes to them receives many curses.

Proverbs 28:27

Cast your bread upon the waters, for after many days you will find it again.

Ecclesiastes 11:1

Heal the sick, raise the dead, cleanse those who have leprosy, drive out demons. Freely you have received, freely give.

Matthew 10:8

And everyone who has left houses or brothers or sisters or father or mother or children or fields for my sake will receive a hundred times as much and will inherit eternal life.

Matthew 19:29

Give, and it will be given to you. A good measure, pressed down, shaken together and running over, will be poured into your lap. For with the measure you use, it will be measured to you.

Luke 6:38

On the first day of every week, each one of you should set aside a sum of money in keeping with his income, saving it up, so that when I come no collections will have to be made.

1 Corinthians 16:2

Remember this: Whoever sows sparingly will also reap sparingly, and whoever sows generously will also reap generously.

Each man should give what he has decided in his heart to give, not reluctantly or under compulsion, for God loves a cheerful giver.

And God is able to make all grace abound to you, so that in all things at all times, having all that you need, you will abound in every good work.

2 Corinthians 9:6-8

Command those who are rich in this present world not to be arrogant nor to put their hope in wealth, which is so uncertain, but to put their hope in God, who richly provides us with everything for our enjoyment.

Command them to do good, to be rich in good deeds, and to be generous and willing to share.

In this way they will lay up treasure for themselves as a firm foundation for the coming age, so that they may take hold of the life that is truly life.

1 Timothy 6:17-19

If anyone has material possessions and sees his brother in need but has no pity on him, how can the love of God be in him?

Dear children, let us not love with words or tongue but with actions and in truth.

1 John 3:17,18

Dear friend, I pray that you may enjoy good health and that all may go well with you, even as your soul is getting along well.

3 John 2

≈ *A Godly Example as a Mother* ≈

He did what was right in the eyes of the Lord, just as his father David had done.

2 Chronicles 29:2

He who walks with the wise grows wise, but a companion of fools suffers harm.

Proverbs 13:20

And if anyone gives even a cup of cold water to one of these little ones because he is my disciple, I tell you the truth, he will certainly not lose his reward.

Matthew 10:42

Just as the Son of Man did not come to be served, but to serve, and to give his life as a ransom for many.

Matthew 20:28

Instead, whoever wants to become great among you must be your servant, and whoever wants to be first must be slave of all.

Mark 10:43,44

I have set you an example that you should do as I have done for you.

I tell you the truth, no servant is greater than his master, nor is a messenger greater than the one who sent him.

A new command I give you: Love one another. As I have loved you, so you must love one another.

John 13:15,16,34

May the God who gives endurance and encouragement give you a spirit of unity among yourselves as you follow Christ Jesus, so that with one heart and mouth you may glorify the God and Father of our Lord Jesus Christ.

Accept one another, then, just as Christ accepted you, in order to bring praise to God.

Romans 15:5-7

Now it is required that those who have been given a trust must prove faithful.

1 Corinthians 4:2

Therefore, my dear brothers, stand firm. Let nothing move you. Always give yourselves fully to the work of the Lord, because you know that your labor in the Lord is not in vain.

1 Corinthians 15:58

Carry each other's burdens, and in this way you will fulfill the law of Christ.

Therefore, as we have opportunity, let us do good to all people, especially to those who belong to the family of believers.

Galatians 6:2,10

Be imitators of God, therefore, as dearly loved children and live a life of love, just as Christ loved us and gave himself up for us as a fragrant offering and sacrifice to God.

Ephesians 5:1,2

Slaves, obey your earthly masters with respect and fear, and with sincerity of heart, just as you would obey Christ.

Obey them not only to win their favor when their eye is on you, but like slaves of Christ, doing the will of God from your heart.

Serve wholeheartedly, as if you were serving the Lord, not men.

Ephesians 6:5-7

Your attitude should be the same as that of Christ Jesus:

Who, being in very nature God, did not consider equality with God something to be grasped, but made himself nothing, taking the very nature of a servant, being made in human likeness.

And being found in appearance as a man, he humbled himself and became obedient to death – even death on a cross!

Philippians 2:5-8

Bear with each other and forgive whatever grievances you may have against one another. Forgive as the Lord forgave you.

Slaves, obey your earthly masters in everything; and do it, not only when their eye is on you and to win their favor, but with sincerity of heart and reverence for the Lord.

Colossians 3:13,22

For everything in the world – the cravings of sinful man, the lust of his eyes and the boasting of what he has and does – comes not from the Father but from the world.

1 John 2:16

This is how we know what love is: Jesus Christ laid down his life for us. And we ought to lay down our lives for our brothers.

1 John 3:16

❧ *A Diligent Mother* ❧

*B*ut as for you, be strong and do not give up, for your work will be rewarded.

2 Chronicles 15:7

He who gathers crops in summer is a wise son, but he who sleeps during harvest is a disgraceful son.

Proverbs 10:5

Diligent hands will rule, but laziness ends in slave labor.

Proverbs 12:24

The sluggard craves and gets nothing, but the desires of the diligent are fully satisfied.

Proverbs 13:4

The plans of the diligent lead to profit as surely as haste leads to poverty.

Proverbs 21:5

Do you see a man skilled in his work? He will serve before kings; he will not serve before obscure men.

Proverbs 22:29

The Sovereign Lord is my strength; he makes my feet like the feet of a deer, he enables me to go on the heights.

Habakkuk 3:19a

Do you not say, "Four months more and then the harvest"? I tell you, open your eyes and look at the fields! They are ripe for harvest.

John 4:35

As long as it is day, we must do the work of him who sent me. Night is coming, when no one can work.

John 9:4

Therefore, as we have opportunity, let us do good to all people, especially to those who belong to the family of believers.

Galatians 6:10

I can do everything through him who gives me strength.

Philippians 4:13

We want each of you to show this same diligence to the very end, in order to make your hope sure.

Hebrews 6:11

I know your deeds. See, I have placed before you an open door that no one can shut. I know that you have little strength, yet you have kept my word and have not denied my name.

Revelation 3:8

❧ *An Honest Mother* ❧

---

*N*ow if you obey me fully and keep my covenant, then out of all nations you will be my treasured possession.

Exodus 19:5a

And if you walk in my ways and obey my statutes and commands as David your father did, I will give you a long life.

1 Kings 3:14

Then the Lord said to Satan, "Have you considered my servant Job? There is no one on earth like him; he is blameless and upright, a man who fears God and shuns evil. And he still maintains his integrity, though you incited me against him to ruin him without any reason."

Job 2:3

Blessed is the man who does not walk in the counsel of the wicked or stand in the way of sinners or sit in the seat of mockers.
But his delight is in the law of the Lord, and on his law he meditates day and night.

Psalm 1:1,2

All the ways of the Lord are loving and faithful for those who keep the demands of his covenant.

Psalm 25:10

The fear of the Lord is the beginning of wisdom; all who follow his precepts have good understanding. To him belongs eternal praise.

Psalm 111:10

Blessed are they who keep his statutes and seek him with all their heart. You have laid down precepts that are to be fully obeyed.

Psalm 119:2,4

Vindicate me, O Lord, for I have led a blameless life; I have trusted in the Lord without wavering.

Psalm 26:1

In my integrity you uphold me and set me in your presence forever.

Psalm 41:12

And David shepherded them with integrity of heart; with skillful hands he led them.

Psalm 78:72

The integrity of the upright guides them, but the unfaithful are destroyed by their duplicity.

Proverbs 11:3

Better a poor man whose walk is blameless than a fool whose lips are perverse.
He who obeys instructions guards his life, but he who is contemptuous of his ways will die.

Proverbs 19:1,16

The righteous man leads a blameless life; blessed are his children after him.

Proverbs 20:7

If you are willing and obedient, you will eat the best from the land.

Isaiah 1:19

Do not repay anyone evil for evil. Be careful to do what is right in the eyes of everybody.

Romans 12:17

Finally, brothers, whatever is true, whatever is noble, whatever is right, whatever is pure, whatever is lovely, whatever is admirable – if anything is excellent or praiseworthy – think about such things.

Philippians 4:8

Live such good lives among the pagans that, though they accuse you of doing wrong, they may see your good deeds and glorify God on the day he visits us.

1 Peter 2:12

❧ *A Courageous Mother* ❧

---

*B*e strong and courageous. Do not be afraid or terrified because of them, for the Lord your God goes with you; he will never leave you nor forsake you.

Deuteronomy 31:6

Be strong and courageous, for you will bring the Israelites into the land I promised them on oath, and I myself will be with you.

Deuteronomy 31:23b

Be strong and courageous, because you will lead these people to inherit the land I swore to their forefathers to give them.

Joshua 1:6

David also said to Solomon his son, "Be strong and courageous, and do the work. Do not be afraid or discouraged, for the Lord God, my God, is with you. He will not fail you or forsake you until all the work for the service of the temple of the Lord is finished."

1 Chronicles 28:20

But as for you, be strong and do not give up, for your work will be rewarded.

2 Chronicles 15:7

Be strong and take heart, all you who hope in the Lord.

Psalm 31:24

Counsel and sound judgment are mine; I have understanding and power.

Proverbs 8:14

So do not fear, for I am with you; do not be dismayed, for I am your God. I will strengthen you and help you; I will uphold you with my righteous right hand.

Isaiah 41:10

The Sovereign Lord is my strength; he makes my feet like the feet of a deer, he enables me to go on the heights.

Habakkuk 3:19a

But you will receive power when the Holy Spirit comes on you; and you will be my witnesses in Jerusalem, and in all Judea and Samaria, and to the ends of the earth.

Acts 1:8

And God is able to make all grace abound to you, so that in all things at all times, having all that you need, you will abound in every good work.

2 Corinthians 9:8

Now to him who is able to do immeasurably more than all we ask or imagine, according to his power that is at work within us.

Ephesians 3:20

I can do everything through him who gives me strength.

Philippians 4:13

So do not throw away your confidence; it will be richly rewarded.
You need to persevere so that when you have done the will of God, you will receive what he has promised.

Hebrews 10:35,36

≈ *A Joyful Mother* ≈

---

*L*et the heavens rejoice, let the earth be glad; let them say among the nations, "The Lord reigns!"

1 Chronicles 16:31

You have filled my heart with greater joy than when their grain and new wine abound.

Psalm 4:7

But let all who take refuge in you be glad; let them ever sing for joy. Spread your protection over them, that those who love your name may rejoice in you.

Psalm 5:11

Weeping may remain for a night, but rejoicing comes in the morning.

Psalm 30:5b

Delight yourself in the Lord and he will give you the desires of your heart.

Psalm 37:4

Blessed are those who have learned to acclaim you, who walk in the light of your presence, O Lord.

Psalm 89:15

Shout for joy to the Lord, all the earth.
Worship the Lord with gladness; come before him with joyful songs.
Know that the Lord is God. It is he who made us, and we are his; we are his people, the sheep of his pasture.
Enter his gates with thanksgiving and his courts with praise; give thanks to him and praise his name.

Psalm 100:1-4

Those who sow in tears will reap with songs of joy.

Psalm 126:5

A happy heart makes the face cheerful, but heartache crushes the spirit.

Proverbs 15:13

A cheerful heart is good medicine, but a crushed spirit dries up the bones.

Proverbs 17:22

You will go out in joy and be led forth in peace; the mountains and hills will burst into song before you, and all the trees of the field will clap their hands.

Isaiah 55:12

Though the fig tree does not bud and there are no grapes on the vines, though the olive crop fails and the fields produce no food, though there are no sheep in the pen and no cattle in the stalls, yet I will rejoice in the Lord, I will be joyful in God my Savior.

Habakkuk 3:17,18

However, do not rejoice that the spirits submit to you, but rejoice that your names are written in heaven.

Luke 10:20

May the God of hope fill you with all joy and peace as you trust in him, so that you may overflow with hope by the power of the Holy Spirit.

Romans 15:13

But the fruit of the Spirit is love, joy, peace, patience, kindness, goodness, faithfulness.

Galatians 5:22

Speak to one another with psalms, hymns and spiritual songs. Sing and make music in your heart to the Lord.

Ephesians 5:19

We write this to make our joy complete.

1 John 1:4

≈ *A Good Listener as a Mother* ≈

---

*L*et the wise listen and add to their learning, and let the discerning get guidance – for understanding proverbs and parables, the sayings and riddles of the wise.

The fear of the Lord is the beginning of knowledge, but fools despise wisdom and discipline.

Listen, my son, to your father's instruction and do not forsake your mother's teaching.

Proverbs 1:5-8

The heart of the discerning acquires knowledge; the ears of the wise seek it out.

Proverbs 18:15

The man said to me, "Son of man, look with your eyes and hear with your ears and pay attention to everything I am going to show you."

Ezekiel 40:4a

But everyone who hears these words of mine and does not put them into practice is like a foolish man who built his house on sand.

The rain came down, the streams rose, and the winds blew and beat against that house, and it fell with a great crash.

Matthew 7:26,27

But blessed are your eyes because they see, and your ears because they hear.

Matthew 13:16

Therefore consider carefully how you listen. Whoever has will be given more; whoever does not have, even what he thinks he has will be taken from him.

Luke 8:18

He who listens to you listens to me; he who rejects you rejects me; but he who rejects me rejects him who sent me.

Luke 10:16

He who belongs to God hears what God says. The reason you do not hear is that you do not belong to God.

John 8:47

"You are a king, then!" said Pilate. Jesus answered, "You are right in saying I am a king. In fact, for this reason I was born, and for this I came into the world, to testify to the truth. Everyone on the side of truth listens to me."

John 18:37

Do not merely listen to the word, and so deceive yourselves. Do what it says.

James 1:22

Anyone who listens to the word but does not do what it says is like a man who looks at his face in a mirror.

James 1:23

But the man who looks intently into the perfect law that gives freedom, and continues to do this, not forgetting what he has heard, but doing it – he will be blessed in what he does.

James 1:25

He who has an ear, let him hear what the Spirit says to the churches.

Revelation 2:29

"There are 1,440 opportunities every day to succeed. That is how many minutes there are in each day. I find that putting God first in my day enables me to use my time wisely and accomplish the goals that I have set. It is He Who gives me the wisdom to plan my day, the intelligence to carry out each task, and the energy to do it. And then He gives me the joy and satisfaction of achievement.".

Marilyn Hickey

WHOLESOME FAMILY
RELATIONSHIPS

"WARMING THE NEST"

BY MARILYN HICKEY

*O*ne of the best things that parents can do for their children is to develop the right atmosphere in the home, or what I call "warm the nest."

Frequently we find that even though we are Christians and have a good relationship with the Lord, our home situation is not a warm one. Many times both mates are saved, but just because both are born again does not mean that there is a warm family situation. With this in mind, I would like to discuss how to warm your own home life.

If there is anything that Satan likes to do, it is to knock around a Christian home, causing contention and division. Perhaps your home does not have the joy and abundance of life it is supposed to have in Jesus. When the truth comes forth, it brings light into any situation. As the Word goes forth, I believe it will not only bring light into your home life, but it will also help you to help others to warm their nests too!

✍ *Responsibility in the Christian Home* ✍

---

*O*ne time my daughter Sarah said to me, "Mother, you know at camp this year I went forward because I felt like I didn't have the assurance that I was saved. But I don't want people to know about it because it could look bad on us."

I said to her, "Sarah, I don't care how it looks. The important thing is your relationship to God. It really doesn't matter what other people say. It matters that we please Him; that's the most important thing."

And I believe the same thing about our home relationships. It doesn't matter what people say. It matters whether we please God, and there is only one way to please Him – by faith in His Word.

We must look to what God's Word says about our situation rather than what we see happening around us. Frequently, when everything is going wrong in our family relationships we tend to look for someone to blame. "What's happening in my home?" we ask. "It's my wife! If she weren't such a nag, we'd have good family relationships." Or we say, "It's my husband! If he weren't such a bum, we'd have a marvelous home." Or perhaps, "It's that rebellious son (or daughter) of ours! If it weren't for him, we'd have a peaceful home."

We always like to put the cause of our disharmony in the home on some other member in the family. But the Bible teaches us that we set the atmosphere in the home, and we do that by taking the Word of God and praying and confessing it for our home.

You are the one to set the atmosphere in your home – not your mate, not your children, and not the devil. Don't say, "Well, it's circumstances." **You have power over circumstances!**

～ *Warming Your Nest* ～

---

*H*ere is a scriptural technique for warming your nest:
   The first step is for **you** to **make the communication** (the fellowship, the embracing) **of your faith for your household effectual** (energetic) **by acknowledging who everyone in your household is in Jesus Christ.**

Every member of your household who is born again is a begotten one, a saint. You need to acknowledge that fact by your confession and by the way you treat them. You need to treat them with respect. I'm not saying that you shouldn't discipline your children, or that they shouldn't do the dishes or pick up their clothes; but you shouldn't talk to them in a condescending way to get it done.

The second step is for you to identify with your family members. In his letter to Philemon, Paul refers to one of his disciples, Onesimus, as his son:

...my son Onesimus, whom I have begotten in my bonds: which in time past was to thee unprofitable, but now profitable to thee

and to me: whom I have sent again: thou therefore receive him, that is, mine own bowels.

Philemon 10-12, KJV

Paul obviously had a strong affection for Onesimus. He called him his son, his bowels, himself. He identified totally with him. Do the same for your loved ones. Identify with them. Become totally one with them.

The third step is for **you** to **acknowledge and appreciate the worth of your family members.** Onesimus was a runaway slave of Philemon's whom Paul had met and led to the Lord. The name *Onesimus* means "profitable." Here Paul writes to Philemon that while Onesimus was once an unprofitable slave and a thief, now he is truly profitable both to Paul and to his master Philemon.

Did you know that your children were profitable? Not only profitable to the Lord, but also profitable to you! Sometimes I think that the sweetest lessons in faith that I have learned have come from my children.

One time our family was confessing together and releasing our faith for a particular thing to take place. We had confessed this event for a whole month. Finally one day my son Mike walked up to me and said, "Mother, where is that thing we have confessed for?"

I was glad to hear that he was interested, so I told him, "We didn't say it was to be here by the first of the month, but by the end of the month."

"Oh," he said, "then we are still expecting it."

"We are receiving it," I said.

Begin to have your family confess things together with you, and you will find that they are profitable.

The final step is for **you** to **express confidence in your family members.** Did you ever say to your mate or your children, "I have confidence in you. You'll do well"? That is such a key thing. That is making your faith effectual by acknowledging what your household is in Christ Jesus. If anyone ever taught me that by a visual aid, it was my mother.

I can remember coming home from school when I was in the first grade and saying, "Oh, Mother, I'd really like to get all A's on my spelling tests, but I don't know if I can." She'd say, "Of course, you can. I know you can." I remember thinking, *If my mother thinks that, then I must be able.* Throughout my school years whenever I'd go to her all "up-tight" and say, "Mother, I don't know if I can handle this," she would always say, "Of course, you can. I know you can. You've always done well, and you always will." I used to think that she was prejudiced, but now I know she was moving in faith!

There was a specific time in college when I could have gotten into deep sinful difficulties, and I almost did. The night that I was involved in this thing, something happened and I didn't get caught up in it. Two weeks later when I was home I told my mother about it. I was nineteen at the time. I said, "Mother, I feel like I've let you down. You've always had such confidence in me."

"Marilyn," she replied, "that doesn't bother me anymore than if you had said you hurt your little finger. I still have confidence in you."

You don't know what that did for me! Her confidence in me kept me out of trouble many times when I could have easily gotten into it.

Later on, Mother asked me what time it was that this temptation had come. Then without waiting for my answer, she asked, "At such-and-such a time on Friday night"?

"Yes," I said.

She then told me, "The Lord woke me that night and told me to get out of bed. I prayed in the Spirit for you."

She made her faith effectual by acknowledging what God had in me. You can do the same thing by acknowledging what God has in your children and your mate.

What do you confess for your mate? "Aw, that bum! Always grouchy; always nasty! Steady disposition – always hateful!" Or do you confess who your family members are in Christ Jesus and who He is in them? Remember, faith is not what you see. Faith is what you **know** to be true from the Word.

I have noticed that as I have confessed the Word about my son and my daughter, they have begun to act upon my confession. Mike is a wise son, a totally committed man of God. Sarah is a wise daughter, and she pleases her father.

You might say, "Marilyn, do you always see that?" No, I don't see it with the natural eye all the time, but that's when I confess it the most! Make your faith effectual by acknowledging every good thing that God has in your household. You'll warm your nest and change it from being a cold, indifferent situation into a victorious, harmonious place of peace and joy.

Our nests should be the warmest – the best! I think that Christian mates should have the best relationship of all. Did Jesus come to give us a life of disaster? Or did He come to give us life in abundance? The last verse of Malachi says that in the last days the Lord **shall turn the heart of the fathers to the children, and the heart of the children to their fathers** (Mal. 4:6, KJV). We need to quote that for our families and make it effectual.

Jesus has never called us to criticize; He has called us to edify, to build up. *If you sincerely want to see your family and home life changed and transformed by the Word, then make this prayer confession with me:*

Father, I know that the power of life and death is in my tongue; Your Word says so. I know that I am an instrument either to build or to destroy.

Right now I enter into a covenant with You that no corrupt communication is going to come out my mouth against my mate, against my children, or against the Church which is the Body of Christ. I am going to live to edify and to build, not to destroy.

Your Word says that I quench every fiery dart that the enemy fires against me by my faith. I take the Word of faith, and I put out the fire of the devil right now. There is no weapon formed against my home, against my relationship with my mate or my children that shall prosper. Every weapon shall go down, in the name of Jesus. I thank You that it is my heritage to put down weapons of the enemy, to put down tongues of condemnation, for righteousness is of the Lord.

I am the righteousness of God right now. Thank You for our warm nest that produces the best people who are totally committed to You. In Jesus' name. Amen.

DEVELOPING PROPER
RELATIONSHIPS SCRIPTURES

❧ *With Your Spouse* ❧

*M*arriage should be honored by all, and the marriage bed kept pure, for God will judge the adulterer and all the sexually immoral.

Hebrews 13:4

A wife of noble character is her husband's crown, but a disgraceful wife is like decay in his bones.

Proverbs 12:4

Her children arise and call her blessed; her husband also, and he praises her. Her husband has full confidence in her and lacks nothing of value.

Proverbs 31:28,11

But since there is so much immorality, each man should have his own wife, and each woman her own husband.

The husband should fulfill his marital duty to his wife, and likewise the wife to her husband.

The wife's body does not belong to her alone but also to her husband. In the same way, the husband's body does not belong to him alone but also to his wife.

To the married I give this command (not I, but the Lord): A wife must not separate from her husband.

But if she does, she must remain unmarried or else be reconciled to her husband. And a husband must not divorce his wife.

And if a woman has a husband who is not a believer and he is willing to live with her, she must not divorce him.

For the unbelieving husband has been sanctified through his wife, and the unbelieving wife has been sanctified through her believing husband. Otherwise your children would be unclean, but as it is, they are holy.

A woman is bound to her husband as long as he lives. But if her husband dies, she is free to marry anyone she wishes, but he must belong to the Lord.

1 Corinthians 7:2-4,10,11,13,14,39

However, each one of you also must love his wife as he loves himself, and the wife must respect her husband.

Ephesians 5:33

Wives, submit to your husbands as to the Lord.

For the husband is the head of the wife as Christ is the head of the church, his body, of which he is the Savior.

Now as the church submits to Christ, so also wives should submit to their husbands in everything.

Husbands, love your wives, just as Christ loved the church and gave himself up for her.

Ephesians 5:22-25

Wives, submit to your husbands, as is fitting in the Lord.

Husbands, love your wives and do not be harsh with them.

Colossians 3:18,19

Then they can train the younger women to love their husbands and children,

To be self-controlled and pure, to be busy at home, to be kind, and to be subject to their husbands, so that no one will malign the word of God.

Titus 2:4,5

Wives, in the same way be submissive to your husbands so that, if any of them do not believe the word, they may be won over without words by the behavior of their wives.

For this is the way the holy women of the past who put their hope in God used to make themselves beautiful. They were submissive to their own husbands.

Husbands, in the same way be considerate as you live with your wives, and treat them with respect as the weaker partner and as heirs with you of the gracious gift of life, so that nothing will hinder your prayers.

1 Peter 3:1,5,7

Your wife will be like a fruitful vine within your house; your sons will be like olive shoots around your table.

Psalm 128:3

May your fountain be blessed, and may you rejoice in the wife of your youth.

Proverbs 5:18

Houses and wealth are inherited from parents, but a prudent wife is from the Lord.

Proverbs 19:14

Enjoy life with your wife, whom you love, all the days of this meaningless life that God has given you under the sun – all your meaningless days. For this is your lot in life and in your toilsome labor under the sun.

Ecclesiastes 9:9

With Your Children

---

*H*e settles the barren woman in her home as a happy mother of children. Praise the Lord.

Psalm 113:9

Remember the day you stood before the Lord your God at Horeb, when he said to me, "Assemble the people before me to hear my words so that they may learn to revere me as long as they live in the land and may teach them to their children."

Deuteronomy 4:10

These commandments that I give you today are to be upon your hearts. Impress them on your children. Talk about them when you sit at home and when you walk along the road, when you lie down and when you get up.

Deuteronomy 6:6,7

Fix these words of mine in your hearts and minds; tie them as symbols on your hands and bind them on your foreheads. Teach them to your children, talking about them when you sit at home and when you walk along the road, when you lie down and when you get up.

Deuteronomy 11:18,19

Jesus said, "Let the little children come to me, and do not hinder them, for the kingdom of heaven belongs to such as these."

Matthew 19:14

Whoever welcomes one of these little children in my name welcomes me; and whoever welcomes me does not welcome me but the one who sent me.

Mark 9:37

If you then, though you are evil, know how to give good gifts to your children, how much more will your Father in heaven give the Holy Spirit to those who ask him!

Luke 11:13

If you, then, though you are evil, know how to give good gifts to your children, how much more will your Father in heaven give good gifts to those who ask him!

Matthew 7:11

The promise is for you and your children and for all who are far off – for all whom the Lord our God will call.

Acts 2:39

For the unbelieving husband has been sanctified through his wife, and the unbelieving wife has been sanctified through her believing husband. Otherwise your children would be unclean, but as it is, they are holy.

1 Corinthians 7:14

Now I am ready to visit you for the third time, and I will not be a burden to you, because what I want is not your possessions but you. After all, children should not have to save up for their parents, but parents for their children.

2 Corinthians 12:14

Children, obey your parents in the Lord, for this is right.

"Honor your father and mother" – which is the first commandment with a promise –

"That it may go well with you and that you may enjoy long life on the earth."

Fathers, do not exasperate your children; instead, bring them up in the training and instruction of the Lord.

Ephesians 6:1-4

Children, obey your parents in everything, for this pleases the Lord.

Fathers, do not embitter your children, or they will become discouraged.

Colossians 3:20,21

For you know that we dealt with each of you as a father deals with his own children.

1 Thessalonians 2:11

He must manage his own family well and see that his children obey him with proper respect.

A deacon must be the husband of but one wife and must manage his children and his household well.

1 Timothy 3:4,12

An elder must be blameless, the husband of but one wife, a man whose children believe and are not open to the charge of being wild and disobedient.

Titus 1:6

Then they can train the younger women to love their husbands and children.

Titus 2:4

✑ *With Your Parents* ✑

Children, obey your parents in the Lord, for this is right.

Ephesians 6:1

Children, obey your parents in everything, for this pleases the Lord.

Colossians 3:20

Do not rebuke an older man harshly, but exhort him as if he were your father. Treat younger men as brothers,

Older women as mothers, and younger women as sisters, with absolute purity.

1 Timothy 5:1,2

But if a widow has children or grandchildren, these should learn first of all to put their religion into practice by caring for their own family and so repaying their parents and grandparents, for this is pleasing to God.

The widow who is really in need and left all alone puts her hope in God and continues night and day to pray and to ask God for help.

But the widow who lives for pleasure is dead even while she lives.

Give the people these instructions, too, so that no one may be open to blame.

If anyone does not provide for his relatives, and especially for his immediate family, he has denied the faith and is worse than an unbeliever.

No widow may be put on the list of widows unless she is over sixty, has been faithful to her husband,

And is well known for her good deeds, such as bringing up children, showing hospitality, washing the feet of the saints, helping those in trouble and devoting herself to all kinds of good deeds.

1 Timothy 5:4-10

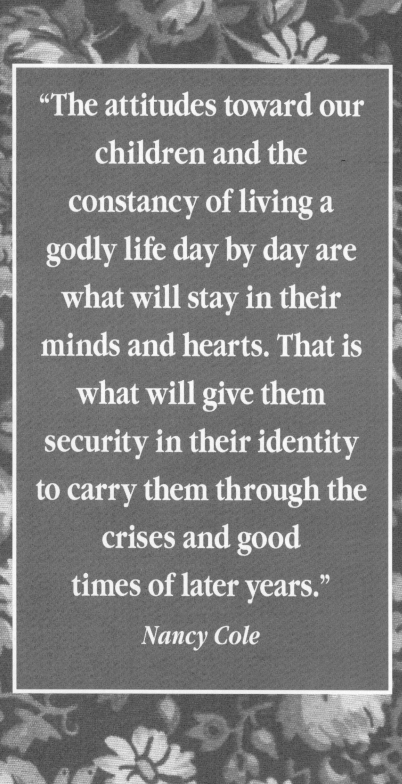

"The attitudes toward our children and the constancy of living a godly life day by day are what will stay in their minds and hearts. That is what will give them security in their identity to carry them through the crises and good times of later years."

Nancy Cole

MOTHERHOOD AND CAREER

11

"TWO CHOICES – BUSINESS AND MOTHER"

BY ED & NANCY COLE

*W*hile contemplating ministry in the home and motherhood, I happened to be on the telephone talking to my daughter, Lois. She and her husband, Rick, have given us two of the most beautiful, brilliant, loveable and enjoyable granddaughters the world has ever seen. And if you think I am prejudiced, you are right!

While I was talking to her, I asked her what being a mother meant to her. This was her reply: "Being a mother means never having a free moment even on vacations. It means being responsible for little people twenty-four hours a day with never a day off."

I chimed in with the observation that even when our children are in their thirties, as Lois is, the responsibility is still there. We both laughed. She and I enjoy motherhood. I do not know of anyone who enjoys her children more or is a better mother without stress or strain than Lois. However, the fact of the matter is that we touched on a sober reality: motherhood is a full-time job that never ends! Being a mother is a great and awesome responsibility. Many of us get married and can hardly wait for that first baby. All we can think of is that soft, warm, tiny mass of humanity.

What women usually do not think about are the sleepless nights, the mounds of dirty diapers, the feeding difficulties, the colic, and all those other unpleasant things that rear their ugly heads during the course of infancy and the toddler stage.

"Will this ever end?" may be a mother's cry! The answer is obvious. Barring calamity, no, it will never end. But the joys of motherhood far outweigh the burden of responsibility.

Mothers imprint their attitudes and ideas onto the child's young, immature life. So it is very important what we are putting into that child. Are you implanting a fearful, critical attitude or a peaceful, loving, forgiving, God-fearing nature?

When my children were young, I guess I made every mistake a new mother can make. I am sure I was short-tempered at times. None of us is perfect. But *it is what we do with our failures that counts*. Do we take them to the Lord and ask for forgiveness? Do we ask our children to forgive us when necessary?

Our attitudes toward the children and the constancy of living a godly life day by day are what will stay in their minds and hearts. That is what will give them a security in their identity to carry them through the crises and good times of later years. Providing you have worked on putting a God-consciousness into their spirits, they will have the marvelous assurance of who they are in God.

Also remember that each of your children has a different, unique personality. When Paul, as a young teenager, spent hours playing the guitar in his room, I had no idea he was composing songs that later blessed our congregation and others with their purity and simplicity.

Nor did I recognize Lois' propensity for debate (which sometimes we called "arguing") that presaged a successful career as a prosecuting attorney.

With Joann, I remember seeing her tie her shoes at a very early age, before kindergarten, and I was ashamed that I had not even tried to teach her that skill which she learned by herself. Then in fifth grade, there was talk of skipping her to seventh grade. I realized she was smart, but what I did not realize was her extraordinary sensitivity to the world around her. Not until she was through school and going through a turbulent time spiritually did I develop an awareness that she, and the other children were made up of spirit, soul and body, each uniquely different from the others.

My children still surprise me with some of the qualities they exhibit. I think, "Where did they ever learn that?" We have to remember we may not always see our children as they really are in God's eyes. We must discipline ourselves in prayer to learn what "makes them tick."

Edwin and I do not have a perfect family, but we have stayed on our knees and God has been faithful. If you think you, or your children, cannot live up to God's greatest goals for your lives, quit trying to do it on your own. Let God be strong within you, instead of trying to be strong for Him. We cannot impress God. But we are impressed by Him when we see what He makes of our lives. Release your children to God and allow them to achieve.

My daughters have struggled with being working mothers as I did. I have noticed, however, that every woman in Scripture worked or held some kind of title, although not always for pay. Every mother must examine her own heart about working outside the home, whether as a volunteer or for pay. What a fallacy to call a full-time homemaker a nonworking mother!

There are women who prefer outside involvement, even though they do not have to work. The Bible certainly teaches it is better to be busy than idle and that godly women adorn themselves with good works. Idleness leads to gossip. It also leads to fantasy and sexual immorality. So the choice of occupying yourself with work or not is up to you, although the priorities of family first never change.

If you find yourself in the workplace earning a living for any reason, then by all means, get the best job possible, preferably one with a chance for advancement. If you have the talent and brains for a high-level job and the opportunity is there, then go for it! If you have to be away from your family anyway, at least make those hours worth your time, and theirs.

There is a pitfall in career planning, however, which you will have to keep in balance – and that is the cost to your family.

Lois was in line for a promotion but in observing the people already in that coveted post, she saw this would be a very time-consuming position that would require long hours both in the office and at home. She had had a taste of this occasionally and it troubled her. Once when she was engaged in some extra, very intensive work, she told me that even though she would go home to be with her family, she was so preoccupied, she would not hear them when they attempted to converse with her. In one instance her troubled little girl said, "Mom! I have asked you the same question five times, and you didn't hear me even once."

When the time came for the promotion, Lois very prayerfully and conscientiously turned it down. Since then, she and Rick have moved to an entirely new community where their workplaces are closer to home and their daughters' schools, and Lois is in an even more exciting position! God does lead and guide us, as He has promised in His Word.

Whether you are working or not, every mother wonders at times if she is losing patience or sanity. A few years ago, I was visiting my son when his youngest child was barely three years old. My daughter-in-law, Judi, was being a lovely hostess and making sure I was comfortable.

The first morning she scurried around the kitchen serving waffles to us all. When she handed me my plate, I looked down at a sight that would make a pre-schooler drool: buttered waffles covered with syrup and cut into bite-sized pieces. When Judi saw me hesitate, she looked at the plate and realized what she had done. We all laughed uproariously. Cutting everyone's food is the classic blooper of a mother of small children!

Judi found that being home continually with her children caused her mind to stagnate and her social skills to diminish. So she worked sporadically, choosing her own hours as a makeup artist, and finally started a business out of her own house. Now she is able to be with the children but have outside interests as well.

A mother with young children must be careful lest the cares of the world choke the life, or spirit, out of her. When the pressure is on, it is easy to develop bad habits. One of those is to take out frustrations on the children. We must learn to accept our weaknesses as ours and not blame the children because we have let anxiety or pressure mount.

On the other hand, we cannot wait and let the father deal with the more serious issues. "Just wait until your father gets home!" is a phrase that, with a little bit of contemplation and calmness, could so often be avoided. A working father comes home from a turbulent world wanting a peaceful haven. He does not need his children dreading his return home, nor does he need a blow-by-blow account of every detail of the day.

The relationship with your children must never become a stumbling block to the relationship with your husband. Children need the benefits of a good marriage between their father and mother.

A common complaint among young mothers is the massive amount of work — cleaning up after more and more people in the house, mounds of laundry, hungry mouths to feed three times a day. Most young mothers lead strenuous lives. But if you plan carefully, and train the children (and your husband!) to help, you can do it. I was surprised to read a doctor's report suggesting that by eight years of age children should be responsible for cleaning their own bedrooms, and by ten they should be able to do any major chore around the house, even vacuuming.

I discovered this for myself when my children were very small. Many a night as we pioneered a new church with three children under four years of age, I crawled into bed on legs that felt hollowed out and barely functionable. I will never forget the feeling! Then Edwin began ministering as a missionary-evangelist and was frequently away on trips that lasted days, weeks, and sometimes months. To add to the difficulty of being alone with the children, I worked full time and drove an hour each way to work. Those were not easy years, but God gave me wisdom.

I realized that if I wanted the children to help me with chores when they were older, I might as well start right then. (Later I discovered this was scriptural! – Hebrews 12:11.) So on Saturday mornings, they each had an assignment. Even the youngest at five years old had a dust cloth and dusted the entire house herself. Granted, I had to go behind them and pick up what they missed after they were in bed at night, but after a few years of investing this way, I reaped big dividends. They all became valuable helps to me around the house.

There is only one regret that remains from those years, and that is when Paul showed an interest in cooking, I did not teach him. (Yes, I confess to stereotyped thinking!) Not only did I live to regret stifling that creative outlet, but so does his wife, Judi!

Another thing God showed me during that time was how to spend time alone with Him regardless of how full my days were. The plan He gave me was both simple and effective once I implemented it. Here it is: I put the children to bed earlier!

I knew Paul had a flashlight under his covers and he was reading, and I could hear Lois and Joann giggling. Nevertheless, I was marvelously alone for a few quiet moments in the evenings to enjoy the Lord – just Him and me. That relationship is the most important to keep intact.

As Edwin says, "It is more important to talk to the Lord about your children than to your children about the Lord."

One more thing I want to add: Did you ever treat your child or children in a way you had vowed never to treat them? Perhaps your parents treated you that way, and long ago you vowed you would never do the same thing. If this has happened to you, examine your heart for unforgiveness toward your parents. You may hardly be aware of the resentment that you still feel over those incidents that disturbed you. When you become aware of hidden resentments, you can be released by forgiving those who hurt you, whether they are still living or not, and asking the Lord to take it out of your life.

Overall, it is your attitude toward your child that will linger on. An attitude of appreciation toward children is what I suggest as the antidote for attitudes of resentment, jealousy, or frustration. Choose to appreciate the great attributes God has placed within the life of each one.

Thank God every day for your husband and/or children. They are His gifts to you. Thank Him for your home. Thank Him for the peace that He floods your heart with. Psalm 91, Isaiah 65:24, John 15:7, 1 Chronicles 16:11, Psalm 25:5, and Isaiah 30:15 are great scriptures to start the day with as you prepare to minister in the home.

YOUR WORK SCRIPTURES

 When You Must Balance Family and Career

*H*e must manage his own family well and see that his children obey him with proper respect.

(If anyone does not know how to manage his own family, how can he take care of God's church?)

1 Timothy 3:4,5

If anyone does not provide for his relatives, and especially for his immediate family, he has denied the faith and is worse than an unbeliever.

1 Timothy 5:8

Only be careful, and watch yourselves closely so that you do not forget the things your eyes have seen or let them slip from your heart as long as you live. Teach them to your children and to their children after them.

Deuteronomy 4:9

He decreed statutes for Jacob and established the law in Israel, which he commanded our forefathers to teach their children, so the next generation would know them, even the children yet to be born, and they in turn would tell their children.

Psalm 78:5,6

Teach us to number our days aright, that we may gain a heart of wisdom.

Psalm 90:12

Blessed are all who fear the Lord, who walk in his ways.
You will eat the fruit of your labor; blessings and prosperity will be yours.
Your wife will be like a fruitful vine within your house; your sons will be like olive shoots around your table.
Thus is the man blessed who fears the Lord.

Psalm 128:1-4

The sluggard craves and gets nothing, but the desires of the diligent are fully satisfied.

Proverbs 13:4

In his heart a man plans his course, but the Lord determines his steps.

Proverbs 16:9

The righteous man leads a blameless life; blessed are his children after him.

Proverbs 20:7

Train a child in the way he should go, and when he is old he will not turn from it.

Proverbs 22:6

By wisdom a house is built, and through understanding it is established.

Proverbs 24:3

Discipline your son, and he will give you peace; he will bring delight to your soul.

Proverbs 29:17

A wife of noble character who can find? She is worth far more than rubies.
Her husband has full confidence in her and lacks nothing of value.
She brings him good, not harm, all the days of her life.
She selects wool and flax and works with eager hands.
She is like the merchant ships, bringing her food from afar.
She gets up while it is still dark; she provides food for her family and portions for her servant girls.

She considers a field and buys it; out of her earnings she plants a vineyard. She sets about her work vigorously; her arms are strong for her tasks.

She sees that her trading is profitable, and her lamp does not go out at night. In her hand she holds the distaff and grasps the spindle with her fingers. She opens her arms to the poor and extends her hands to the needy.

When it snows, she has no fear for her household; for all of them are clothed in scarlet.

She makes coverings for her bed; she is clothed in fine linen and purple.

Her husband is respected at the city gate, where he takes his seat among the elders of the land.

She makes linen garments and sells them, and supplies the merchants with sashes.

She is clothed with strength and dignity; she can laugh at the days to come.

She speaks with wisdom, and faithful instruction is on her tongue. She watches over the affairs of her household and does not eat the bread of idleness.

Her children arise and call her blessed; her husband also, and he praises her: "Many women do noble things, but you surpass them all."

Charm is deceptive, and beauty is fleeting; but a woman who fears the Lord is to be praised.

Proverbs 31:10-30

All your sons will be taught by the Lord, and great will be your children's peace.

In righteousness you will be established: Tyranny will be far from you; you will have nothing to fear. Terror will be far removed; it will not come near you.

Isaiah 54:13,14

But seek first his kingdom and his righteousness, and all these things will be given to you as well.

Matthew 6:33

Be very careful, then, how you live – not as unwise but as wise, making the most of every opportunity, because the days are evil.

Ephesians 5:15,16

Be wise in the way you act toward outsiders; make the most of every opportunity.

Colossians 4:5

≈ *When You Are Your Family's Sole Support* ≈

*T*he Lord is good, a refuge in times of trouble. He cares for those who trust in him.

Nahum 1:7

Since you are my rock and my fortress, for the sake of your name lead and guide me.

Psalm 31:3

I will instruct you and teach you in the way you should go; I will counsel you and watch over you.

Psalm 32:8

You guide me with your counsel, and afterward you will take me into glory.

Psalm 73:24

For the Lord gives wisdom, and from his mouth come knowledge and understanding.

Proverbs 2:6

Trust in the Lord with all your heart and lean not on your own understanding.

Proverbs 3:5

Lazy hands make a man poor, but diligent hands bring wealth.

Proverbs 10:4

Diligent hands will rule, but laziness ends in slave labor.

Proverbs 12:24

The sluggard craves and gets nothing, but the desires of the diligent are fully satisfied.

Proverbs 13:4

Plans fail for lack of counsel, but with many advisers they succeed.

Proverbs 15:22

Do not love sleep or you will grow poor; stay awake and you will have food to spare.

Proverbs 20:13

Do you see a man skilled in his work? He will serve before kings; he will not serve before obscure men.

Proverbs 22:29

By wisdom a house is built, and through understanding it is established.

Proverbs 24:3

A wife of noble character who can find? She is worth far more than rubies.
She is clothed with strength and dignity; she can laugh at the days to come.
She speaks with wisdom, and faithful instruction is on her tongue.
She watches over the affairs of her household and does not eat the bread of idleness.
Her children arise and call her blessed; her husband also, and he praises her:
"Many women do noble things, but you surpass them all."
Charm is deceptive, and beauty is fleeting; but a woman who fears the Lord is to be praised.
Give her the reward she has earned, and let her works bring her praise at the city gate.

Proverbs 31:10,25-31

Sow your seed in the morning, and at evening let not your hands be idle, for you do not know which will succeed, whether this or that, or whether both will do equally well.

Ecclesiastes 11:6

So do not fear, for I am with you; do not be dismayed, for I am your God. I will strengthen you and help you; I will uphold you with my righteous right hand.

Isaiah 41:10

This is what the Lord says – your Redeemer, the Holy One of Israel: "I am the Lord your God, who teaches you what is best for you, who directs you in the way you should go."

Isaiah 48:17

But seek first his kingdom and his righteousness, and all these things will be given to you as well.

Matthew 6:33

Never be lacking in zeal, but keep your spiritual fervor, serving the Lord.

Romans 12:11

And my God will meet all your needs according to his glorious riches in Christ Jesus.

Philippians 4:19

When You Are Fearful for Your Child's Safety

*T*he Lord is my light and my salvation – whom shall I fear? The Lord is the stronghold of my life – of whom shall I be afraid?

Though an army besiege me, my heart will not fear; though war break out against me, even then will I be confident.

Psalm 27:1,3

He who dwells in the shelter of the Most High will rest in the shadow of the Almighty.

He will cover you with his feathers, and under his wings you will find refuge; his faithfulness will be your shield and rampart.

You will not fear the terror of night, nor the arrow that flies by day, nor the pestilence that stalks in the darkness, nor the plague that destroys at midday.

A thousand may fall at your side, ten thousand at your right hand, but it will not come near you.

Psalm 91:1,4-7

Then no harm will befall you, no disaster will come near your tent.
For he will command his angels concerning you to guard you in all your ways.

Psalm 91:10,11

Great peace have they who love your law, and nothing can make them stumble.

Psalm 119:165

Have no fear of sudden disaster or of the ruin that overtakes the wicked, for the Lord will be your confidence and will keep your foot from being snared.

Proverbs 3:25,26

You will keep in perfect peace him whose mind is steadfast, because he trusts in you.

Isaiah 26:3

So do not fear, for I am with you; do not be dismayed, for I am your God. I will strengthen you and help you; I will uphold you with my righteous right hand.

Isaiah 41:10

In righteousness you will be established: Tyranny will be far from you; you will have nothing to fear. Terror will be far removed; it will not come near you.

Isaiah 54:14

Peace I leave with you; my peace I give you. I do not give to you as the world gives. Do not let your hearts be troubled and do not be afraid.   John 14:27

For you did not receive a spirit that makes you a slave again to fear, but you received the Spirit of sonship. And by him we cry, "Abba, Father."

Romans 8:15

Do not be anxious about anything, but in everything, by prayer and petition, with thanksgiving, present your requests to God.

And the peace of God, which transcends all understanding, will guard your hearts and your minds in Christ Jesus.

Finally, brothers, whatever is true, whatever is noble, whatever is right, whatever is pure, whatever is lovely, whatever is admirable – if anything is excellent or praiseworthy – think about such things.   Philippians 4:6-8

For God did not give us a spirit of timidity, but a spirit of power, of love and of self-discipline.   2 Timothy 1:7

There is no fear in love. But perfect love drives out fear, because fear has to do with punishment. The one who fears is not made perfect in love.

1 John 4:18

≈ *Your Relationship With Your Employer* ≈

---

*S*laves, obey your earthly masters with respect and fear, and with sincerity of heart, just as you would obey Christ.

Obey them not only to win their favor when their eye is on you, but like slaves of Christ, doing the will of God from your heart.

Serve wholeheartedly, as if you were serving the Lord, not men,

Because you know that the Lord will reward everyone for whatever good he does, whether he is slave or free.

Ephesians 6:5-8

Slaves, obey your earthly masters in everything; and do it, not only when their eye is on you and to win their favor, but with sincerity of heart and reverence for the Lord.

Whatever you do, work at it with all your heart, as working for the Lord, not for men,

Since you know that you will receive an inheritance from the Lord as a reward. It is the Lord Christ you are serving.

Colossians 3:22-24

All who are under the yoke of slavery should consider their masters worthy of full respect, so that God's name and our teaching may not be slandered.

Those who have believing masters are not to show less respect for them because they are brothers. Instead, they are to serve them even better, because those who benefit from their service are believers, and dear to them. These are the things you are to teach and urge on them.

1 Timothy 6:1,2

Teach slaves to be subject to their masters in everything, to try to please them, not to talk back to them.

Titus 2:9

Slaves, submit yourselves to your masters with all respect, not only to those who are good and considerate, but also to those who are harsh.

1 Peter 2:18

He who tends a fig tree will eat its fruit, and he who looks after his master will be honored.

Proverbs 27:18

Who then is the faithful and wise servant, whom the master has put in charge of the servants in his household to give them their food at the proper time?

It will be good for that servant whose master finds him doing so when he returns.

I tell you the truth, he will put him in charge of all his possessions.

But suppose that servant is wicked and says to himself, "My master is staying away a long time,"

And he then begins to beat his fellow servants and to eat and drink with drunkards.

The master of that servant will come on a day when he does not expect him and at an hour he is not aware of.

He will cut him to pieces and assign him a place with the hypocrites, where there will be weeping and gnashing of teeth.

Matthew 24:45-51

It will be good for those servants whose master finds them watching when he comes. I tell you the truth, he will dress himself to serve, will have them recline at the table and will come and wait on them.

Luke 12:37

Whoever can be trusted with very little can also be trusted with much, and whoever is dishonest with very little will also be dishonest with much.

Luke 16:10

And if you have not been trustworthy with someone else's property, who will give you property of your own?

Luke 16:12

I tell you the truth, no servant is greater than his master, nor is a messenger greater than the one who sent him.

John 13:16

Now it is required that those who have been given a trust must prove faithful.

1 Corinthians 4:2

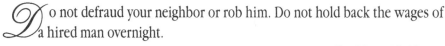

Your Relationship With Your Employees

Do not defraud your neighbor or rob him. Do not hold back the wages of a hired man overnight.

Leviticus 19:13

Do not take advantage of a hired man who is poor and needy, whether he is a brother Israelite or an alien living in one of your towns.

Pay him his wages each day before sunset, because he is poor and is counting on it. Otherwise he may cry to the Lord against you, and you will be guilty of sin.

Deuteronomy 24:14,15

Woe to him who builds his palace by unrighteousness, his upper rooms by injustice, making his countrymen work for nothing, not paying them for their labor.

Jeremiah 22:13

Take no bag for the journey, or extra tunic, or sandals or a staff; for the worker is worth his keep.

Matthew 10:10

Those who have believing masters are not to show less respect for them because they are brothers. Instead, they are to serve them even better, because those who benefit from their service are believers, and dear to them. These are the things you are to teach and urge on them.

1 Timothy 6:2

Now when a man works, his wages are not credited to him as a gift, but as an obligation.

Romans 4:4

And masters, treat your slaves in the same way. Do not threaten them, since you know that he who is both their Master and yours is in heaven, and there is no favoritism with him.

Ephesians 6:9

Masters, provide your slaves with what is right and fair, because you know that you also have a Master in heaven.

Colossians 4:1

For the Scripture says, "Do not muzzle the ox while it is treading out the grain," and "The worker deserves his wages."

1 Timothy 5:18

 ## *Your Daily Schedule Scriptures*
When You Feel Disorganized

---

*S*how me your ways, O Lord, teach me your paths.

Psalm 25:4

I will instruct you and teach you in the way you should go; I will counsel you and watch over you.

Psalm 32:8

Cast your cares on the Lord and he will sustain you; he will never let the righteous fall.

Psalm 55:22

Trust in the Lord with all your heart and lean not on your own understanding; in all your ways acknowledge him, and he will make your paths straight.

Proverbs 3:5,6

In his heart a man plans his course, but the Lord determines his steps.

Proverbs 16:9

Whether you turn to the right or to the left, your ears will hear a voice behind you, saying, "This is the way; walk in it."

Isaiah 30:21

He gives strength to the weary and increases the power of the weak.

Isaiah 40:29

When you pass through the waters, I will be with you; and when you pass through the rivers, they will not sweep over you. When you walk through the fire, you will not be burned; the flames will not set you ablaze.

Isaiah 43:2

Because the Sovereign Lord helps me, I will not be disgraced.

Isaiah 50:7a

For God is not a God of disorder but of peace.

1 Corinthians 14:33a

Do not be anxious about anything, but in everything, by prayer and petition, with thanksgiving, present your requests to God.

And the peace of God, which transcends all understanding, will guard your hearts and your minds in Christ Jesus.

Philippians 4:6,7

If any of you lacks wisdom, he should ask God, who gives generously to all without finding fault, and it will be given to him.

James 1:5

≈ *When Family Devotions Seem Difficult* ≈

*O*nly be careful, and watch yourselves closely so that you do not forget the things your eyes have seen or let them slip from your heart as long as you live. Teach them to your children and to their children after them.

Deuteronomy 4:9

These commandments that I give you today are to be upon your hearts. Impress them on your children. Talk about them when you sit at home and when you walk along the road, when you lie down and when you get up.

Deuteronomy 6:6,7

Fix these words of mine in your hearts and minds; tie them as symbols on your hands and bind them on your foreheads.

Teach them to your children, talking about them when you sit at home and when you walk along the road, when you lie down and when you get up.

Deuteronomy 11:18,19

So the next generation would know them, even the children yet to be born, and they in turn would tell their children.

Then they would put their trust in God and would not forget his deeds but would keep his commands.

Psalm 78:6,7

Blessed are all who fear the Lord, who walk in his ways.

You will eat the fruit of your labor; blessings and prosperity will be yours.

Your wife will be like a fruitful vine within your house; your sons will be like olive shoots around your table.

Thus is the man blessed who fears the Lord.

Psalm 128:1-4

Train a child in the way he should go, and when he is old he will not turn from it.

Proverbs 22:6

By wisdom a house is built, and through understanding it is established.

Proverbs 24:3

Discipline your son, and he will give you peace; he will bring delight to your soul.

Proverbs 29:17

All your sons will be taught by the Lord, and great will be your children's peace.

Isaiah 54:13

Tell it to your children, and let your children tell it to their children, and their children to the next generation.

Joel 1:3

But seek first his kingdom and his righteousness, and all these things will be given to you as well.

Matthew 6:33

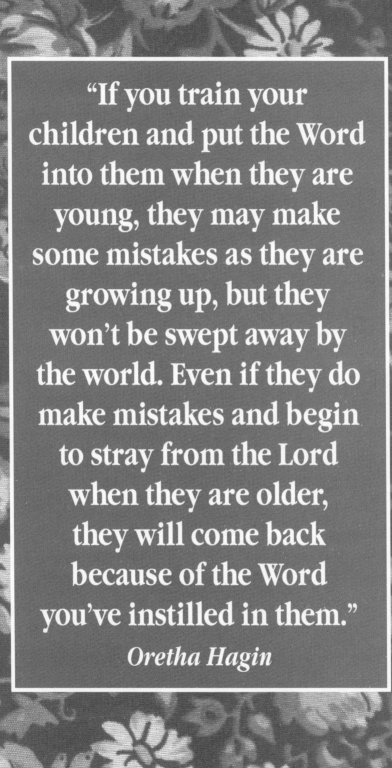

"If you train your children and put the Word into them when they are young, they may make some mistakes as they are growing up, but they won't be swept away by the world. Even if they do make mistakes and begin to stray from the Lord when they are older, they will come back because of the Word you've instilled in them."

Oretha Hagin

FINANCIAL MANAGEMENT

(13)

"HANDLING MONEY"

BY BEA BASANSKY

*T*he husband-wife attitudes toward the handling of the household income and budget need to be in agreement just as much as any other area in their marriage.

"Who should handle the money?" First of all, we cannot lay down any hard and fast rules, as each household is a unique situation. However, we can establish some general principles in line with our basic role as husband or wife.

Have you ever heard a wife say something like this, "We bought this stove with MY money." The immediate implication is a divided financial situation, with two different decision-making "heads" which, nine times out of ten, lead to arguments and for sure play havoc with the male ego.

For the sake of unity, and the fact that the husband is the head of the home, it is best for him to accept his headship in this area and for the household income, checking and savings accounts, to be classified as OUR money. But also, for the sake of harmony in the relationship, it is good for husband and wife to have open communication in this area, to the point that there can be a mutual agreement in HOW you plan to spend and save your money.

Ideally, it is the husband's responsibility to support the family, to provide the money, to manage the main budget, and to make the *final* decisions on how, when and where it is spent. The wife's responsibility should be to support his financial plan and manage the household budget IF he gives it to her to manage. Many men give a portion of the paycheck to their wives – enough to operate the household budget.

I would suggest that he doesn't hand you the whole responsibility of the budget. If he should hand you the responsibility of making the decisions of bill paying, and perhaps trying to decide what to do when there isn't enough money to pay all of the bills or how much should be saved, it could place you in a pressure situation. It may not be realized right away, but after a long period of time it can cause a great deal of resentment in your attitude toward your husband. When he hands you his responsibility, sometimes we as "wife" are deceived into keeping it because we know that we have the ability and educated capability of handling it and doing a good job. However, just because we are capable of doing it doesn't mean it is expedient that we do so.

I would like to insert here that it is good to operate in your God-given role of woman-wife. The world sometimes puts down role playing, but in accordance with God's plan, we have a role as "good wife" to fulfill; otherwise God never would have made a woman and could have just had a world full of "Adams" – He could have just kept creating men at His will. The point is, don't be afraid to fulfill your role, even if you *feel* you are just "role playing." God will honor your faith in doing your part to bring divine order into your home.

If your husband delegates the checkbook responsibility to you, try to see that it remains on a bookkeeping level, where he is making the decisions about what, where and when to pay, and you write the checks and mail them. Let him make the decisions, while you fulfill the role of helpmeet. You are taking on this job to save him the thirty minutes that it often takes to sit down, write the checks out, put them in envelopes, stamp, mail them and keep the checkbook balanced with the bank statement. With an arrangement like this it keeps him in the leadership position. You can still help him with it, but keep your position as his helpmeet. He'll feel better, and you will too.

Some men do all the decision-making and bookkeeping in the household, giving the wife the money she needs to buy groceries, clothing for the family and miscellaneous items. Hopefully, this man even though he is doing all the work on the budget, is taking time to communicate with his wife so that they are in agreement, she is expressing her ideas and ultimately feels she has a part in making this plan work successfully.

Nonetheless, be a dollar stretcher. Help him maintain the budget. Don't mess up the budget because you found a "good deal" at the store today and you just couldn't pass it up! BE A DOLLAR STRETCHER.

Sometimes difference over finances can be solved by making two separate budgets (one for him and one for you). You'll have to discuss this with him, but sometimes this can be the solution to many arguments.

When I had the total responsibility of handling the finances I realized I needed to return Bill's leadership position to him in this area, I had to crucify my pride. I had to say, "Here, Bill, is the checkbook. I realize I have tried to take this financial responsibility away from you and I would like to offer it back to you. We hadn't had a disagreement or anything. I simply had realized what was happening. I wanted him to know I could give it to him to do. I had recognized in my own heart that it was becoming a prideful thing with me and it had also allowed him to release his leadership to me in this area. I admit, there were some reservations in my heart at the beginning, because I thought, "What if he makes a mistake? What if he writes checks and subtracts it and it doesn't balance? What if the statement comes back and something is wrong?" I had to deal with this, these attitudes of lack of faith in him and my pride! It is easier when you are young and haven't had to deal with a lot of poor attitudes and emotions, but older married women who have held this responsibility perhaps for 15 or 20 years, and sometimes without Jesus in their life, will find giving the checkbook back to their husbands a lot harder. However, you need to be willing to do it, knowing that he may make some mistakes. At this point if he does give the checkbook back to you, I'm sure you could accept it on a "helpmeet" basis.

Some of us wives who have been self-centered and prideful are usually right there with our mouth, making sure he has our opinion of how it should be done. "Do it this way, this way, this way!" We stay after them. We don't want them to make any mistakes. We don't want anyone to know he isn't perfect! Let the responsibility be his, it will help him know you have faith and confidence in his leadership ability and it will make him feel good.

Remember this: If God gives *you* the freedom to choose between right and wrong, shouldn't you as a wife be able to allow your husband the freedom to choose right or wrong?

Now, it may be that your husband won't take responsibilities in areas such as this. There are some men who won't. They have been so "hammered down" in their past lives with statements like, "You are going to fail," "You won't make it," or "You don't have it in you." They have had failure ministered to them and it has made them terrified of making mistakes. The male ego part of his soul has been pushed down to such a point that he has no confidence in himself.

If you have been the type of wife who has cut your husband to shreds with your tongue, it means you have a lot of work to do in rebuilding his confidence.

It's a slow process building him up in his soulish area to the point where you can suggest a responsibility here and a responsibility there, that he may be willing to take on.

DON'T NAG! Remember, a nag is someone who says something more than once. Minister to him. It's got to be a *body-soul ministry* on your part. Let the Lord Jesus, through you, restore these things in his life – those areas where he feels he has no confidence. Tell him with your mouth, voice to him (by faith) your confidence in him and point out to him all the ways he is successful and pleasing to you and your family. Then, once he does start taking responsibilities, be sure to tell him how much you appreciate him taking that responsibility off your shoulders. For instance, tell him what a good provider he is. It took me 20 years of married life before I was free enough in my soul to say with my mouth, "Honey, you've been a good provider."

Even when we were in the world, my husband always took good care of us as far as material things were concerned. He always provided enough to keep the bills paid. Everything was always taken care of one way or another. He was a good provider. But never, not once did I ever say with my mouth, "I really appreciate the fact that you have been a good provider in our home." When I realized what I had been doing (or rather, not doing), I went to my husband and said, "I really appreciate the way you've been a good provider for us all of our married life." He was like a little boy. He just "ate up my words," because he appreciated me telling him that. I had thought it in my mind, that I appreciated him, but I had never *given life to the words*. It's just like the Proverb says, your words can either be life or death. It is the little things, in the everyday, common situations in living that you can continuously minister life, or you can continuously minister death.

YOUR FINANCES SCRIPTURES

*B*ut as for you, be strong and do not give up, for your work will be rewarded.

2 Chronicles 15:7

Lazy hands make a man poor, but diligent hands bring wealth.

Proverbs 10:4

Diligent hands will rule, but laziness ends in slave labor.

Proverbs 12:24

The sluggard craves and gets nothing, but the desires of the diligent are fully satisfied.

Proverbs 13:4

Plans fail for lack of counsel, but with many advisers they succeed.

Proverbs 15:22

He who is kind to the poor lends to the Lord, and he will reward him for what he has done.

Proverbs 19:17

Do not love sleep or you will grow poor; stay awake and you will have food to spare.

Proverbs 20:13

Do you see a man skilled in his work? He will serve before kings; he will not serve before obscure men.

Proverbs 22:29

He who works his land will have abundant food, but the one who chases fantasies will have his fill of poverty.

Proverbs 28:19

But seek first his kingdom and his righteousness, and all these things will be given to you as well.

Matthew 6:33

Be sure you know the condition of your flocks, give careful attention to your herds.

Proverbs 27:23

And my God will meet all your needs according to his glorious riches in Christ Jesus.

Philippians 4:19

Dear friend, I pray that you may enjoy good health and that all may go well with you, even as your soul is getting along well.

3 John 2

Honor the Lord with your wealth, with the firstfruits of all your crops; then your barns will be filled to overflowing, and your vats will brim over with new wine.

Proverbs 3:9,10

He who gives to the poor will lack nothing, but he who closes his eyes to them receives many curses.

Proverbs 28:27

Cast your bread upon the waters, for after many days you will find it again.

Ecclesiastes 11:1

"Bring the whole tithe into the storehouse, that there may be food in my house. Test me in this," says the Lord Almighty, "and see if I will not throw open the floodgates of heaven and pour out so much blessing that you will not have room enough for it.

"I will prevent pests from devouring your crops, and the vines in your fields will not cast their fruit," says the Lord Almighty.

Malachi 3:10,11

Give, and it will be given to you. A good measure, pressed down, shaken together and running over, will be poured into your lap. For with the measure you use, it will be measured to you.

Luke 6:38

If anyone has material possessions and sees his brother in need but has no pity on him, how can the love of God be in him?

Dear children, let us not love with words or tongue but with actions and in truth.

1 John 3:17,18

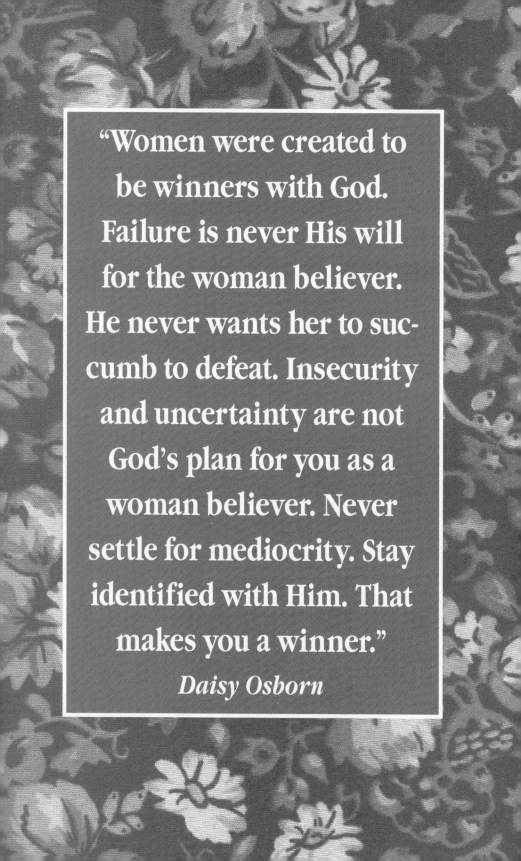

"Women were created to be winners with God. Failure is never His will for the woman believer. He never wants her to succumb to defeat. Insecurity and uncertainty are not God's plan for you as a woman believer. Never settle for mediocrity. Stay identified with Him. That makes you a winner."

Daisy Osborn

VI

PERSONAL MANAGEMENT
AND MATURITY

"ESTABLISHING YOUR PRIORITIES"

BY SHARON DAUGHERTY

*G*od's priorities should be what we seek in life. If we follow His plan, we'll walk with proper balance in both family and ministry responsibilities.

So teach us to number [organize] **our days** [our lives], **that we may apply our hearts unto wisdom.**

Psalm 90:12, KJV

It's important to set priorities in your life. Establish what things are of most importance, then let everything else fall into its right place.

I've found the following to be a helpful guideline for my life. I encourage you to find your own guidelines from the Lord.

Priority No. 1 – time with God.

Priority No. 2 – time with husband.

Priority No. 3 – time with family.

Priority No. 4 – time for ministry.

It should be realized that points two through four will have to be flexible to your priority time with God or you will become a frustrated wife and even resentful to changes. There's peace in being in the right time and in the right place. God will always bless in the other areas where there is flexibility. I've been in this calling long enough to realize this.

～ *Time With God* ～

*W*ife and motherhood duties fall into order as we first submit our ways to God. Time with God is so vital. If we don't have time with Him, we won't be filled up to handle the day effectively. It's like gassing up your car. If you're on "E" and you don't fill up with gas, you'll run out of gas along the way. I know, because I've done it before.

Spiritually speaking, you'll run out of patience, joy, peace, and self-control and will miss God's leading in areas. However, if you start your day with prayer and God's Word you will have on the armor of God, your spirit will be filled with the Holy Spirit's fruits, and your heart will be sensitive to hear God's voice speaking to you. I have a prayer guide which I pray through, and I cover every area that surrounds my life.

When you pray daily, always pray for your husband. Pray that he be filled with God's wisdom, that he be strengthened in his spirit, soul, and body and guarded from the lust of the flesh, the lust of the eyes, and the pride of life. Pray God's Word over him, over yourself, and over your children. Pray God's Word over your ministry and the people of your church. You'll see results!

Take time to read and study God's Word, even if it's only a few minutes. Don't let the devil talk you out of it. That's exactly what he wants to do, so you'll be weak and can't fight him. Remember, you are in a spiritual battle. Keep your guard up.

Many times I have my one hour prayer time when I pray Scripture in the morning. Then I have my Bible reading time in the evening. However you want to do it, just do it. If Jesus had to take time alone with God, then we surely need to.

If your time gets interrupted, don't give up. Sometimes that happens with small children. Just pick up later where you left off. Also, you can pray while you're doing other things if you have to. God wants you to be still and know Him, but there are occasions when you may be interrupted in that time of stillness. This is where flexibility comes in. However, sometimes during your day God will give you time. Be sensitive to take that time with Him.

Whenever I have missed my time at the start of the day, I repented and asked God to forgive me, help me through that day, and help me to get up earlier the next day. That's important, but don't allow condemnation. The devil would love to make you feel like a failure all that day. Don't let him! Draw unto God and resist the devil.

God is looking at your heart. He understands and loves you. Having four small children, I've learned that God understands the life of a mother who is making the effort to seek Him. You can seek Him all through your day. He's listening.

Once I remember when I was feeling weighted down with the care and responsibilities that I had, and God spoke something to my heart. He directed my attention to a Scripture which Jesus spoke to His disciples, **...Come ye yourselves apart into a desert place, and rest a while** (Mark 6:31, KJV).

Jesus and the disciples had been ministering to people, and He realized that as they had "given out of themselves," they needed to be refilled.

God spoke to me, "Sharon, come apart before you come apart." I realized I needed some quality time alone with Him to be built back up, refreshed, restored, and refilled.

Sometimes we'll be able to take time away with our husbands, but there will be those times when we can't take the time away. This was one of the times in my life I knew that I had to draw in to that quiet place in my house with Him.

Oh, the sweetness of His presence when we pour our heart feelings out to Him, cry and laugh and listen to Him speak to our hearts those words of comfort and encouragement.

Your time with God is your source of strength in life. The Word of God also says, **...the joy of the Lord is your strength** (Neh. 8:10, KJV).

I remember the day in my devotion time I was feeling discouraged because of a trial we were going through.

I had been carrying the care of the ministry to the point that I had begun having a physical problem. The Lord showed me that even though I would cast the care on Him at the beginning of my day, later on in the evening when I would be still, I would begin meditating on the care again. This worry caused me to have a slight heart problem.

In my heart He spoke to me to dance before Him, but I just didn't feel like it. He also spoke to my heart that David, the Psalmist, once had to encourage himself in the Lord. (1 Sam. 30:6.) So I began to sing, "The joy of the Lord is my strength" and dance there in my house unto Him. I felt the release within, and He spoke Psalm 40:3 (KJV) to me that He had put a new song in my heart. **And he hath put a new song in my mouth, even praise unto our God.**

Within a couple of weeks, I realized I was healed of my physical problem. You see, carrying the weight of cares can affect your physical body. When you give place to care, fear, unforgiveness, or other such tricks of Satan, you open yourself up for other problems.

It took a process of time to actually walk through the trial, but I had a peace within that God was perfecting the things that concerned us. (Psalm 138:8.) He did!

God began to give me songs as I read the Scriptures. I found that I could rejoice and again rejoice. (Phil. 3:1, 4:4.) Paul had to rejoice continually in the midst of prison situations and trials, and God always delivered him.

It has been said that if we let go of our joy, we let go of our strength. Many times it will be a sacrifice of joy when you begin to rejoice, because you might not feel like it. David, the Psalmist, says to offer up the sacrifice of joy (Psalm 27:6).

You'll sense the grace of God rising up within you to overcome when you rejoice, and His joy will be your strength.

❧ *Time With Husband and Family* ❧

---

*I*t's important that you and your husband take time with each other. Just like any other human being, you need a day off for the family, a day of rest and refreshing. Electricians can tell you if you overload a good circuit too long, it will burn out. We can avoid "burnout" in the ministry by following Scriptural and natural guidelines. Take some time each week for rest and relaxation.

Don't feel condemned to spend time together, just the two of you, maybe for a meal or for a walk. Sometimes it may be late at night before going to bed, but whenever you can, find the time to share together. Also, make time to pray together during your week. If possible, pray together daily. Many times we get up to pray together in our early morning prayer time. Sometimes we've prayed at night before going to bed.

Dr. Edwin Cole has said, "Prayer produces intimacy." We have seen that happen in our lives. You can share things on your heart with each other, and then there also is great power in the prayer of agreement between husband and wife. (Matt. 18:19,20.) Prayer may seem awkward for a husband and wife at first if they've not been praying together before. May I encourage you to press past that awkwardness and into the power of agreement.

Establish time with your children. In order to keep family time, you and your husband may need to mark his calendar for this block of time. There will always be ministry needs, but there will also be needs in your children for time and love. Although you may not have every night free to be at home, the times you have at home can be quality and can meet the needs of your children. Some people have a lot of time at their house but spend it watching TV or with everyone doing their own thing instead of doing something together to build relationships.

Relationships are built by communicating with each other and interacting together. You can find ways to accomplish this as you do things together. Also, as the children grow, include them in your work. Let them feel like they're a part of what you are doing. This also builds relationships with them.

Finally, have family devotion time together (apart from husband and wife prayer time) at some point of the day where you read and then have discussion and pray together. There's an old saying, "The family that prays together stays together." I believe that statement!

At night we have our family devotions. Usually my husband does the Bible reading. Sometimes we talk about it. Then we pray and put the children to bed. This can be interesting when all four children are little! Usually we have some enlightening conversations, too!

⇜ *Time for Ministry* ⇝

ince our calling is ministry and it is not a regular 8:00 to 5:00 job, our time must be flexible with our calling. There are times when we'll be called upon unexpectedly or there will be special services that may go for several nights. Whatever is the case, be flexible and sensitive to the Holy Spirit's leading.

You, as the wife, do not have to go to every meeting within the church, but be sensitive in your spirit to know those you should go to and those which aren't necessary. Pray about when to go and when not to go, and then discuss this with your husband. There are times when my husband and I feel I need to stay home with the children rather than go to a meeting. We can usually tell when the children are tired and need to stay home with Mommy.

Phone calls will come at your house. With all phone calls, always ask immediately who it is and what they need. Sometimes they think the pastor is the only one they can talk to, but many times you or others can handle the matter just as well.

Some of the people can be redirected to staff in the church. Courteously handle and redirect as many of the calls as you can without involving your husband. He needs to feel that when he comes home he can relax with his family.

God may direct you to organize and train some people in your church to do phone counseling. This way, when you receive so many calls, you can redirect some of the calls to others who are on call to help. I have a mercy motive gift and tend to let people talk a lot as I counsel them. There have been times when my husband would come in for supper, the meal would be ready, but he would find me counseling on the phone.

I had to learn how to get people to identify their need, then pray and agree on the Word of God with them and politely excuse myself, letting them know we could talk again at church.

Some people will monopolize your time. I have had to learn how to handle them lovingly, yet firmly, with the help of the Holy Spirit.

We've found a phone recorder to be a great help to us. We put it on when we're away from the house, when we're outside, or when we're eating a meal. This way, we don't miss any phone calls, and we still can have a few minutes of family time together.

Phone recorders have become very common, and most people understand when you need to use them. There will always be some people who don't like them, but these same people rarely understand your need for privacy either. If an emergency arises, you'll have the message on the recorder. Without it, you might not hear of the emergency until too late. Pray about using a recorder to help you.

You may be wondering, "What about time for myself?" This is needed but should remain under submission to God and the other areas of need you have. In our society today, selfishness is so rampant. Time for self should be sandwiched in, in a flexible way where the other areas are not taken from because of it, but added to. For instance, other than my time alone with God I find time to jog one to two miles, four days a week, in the mornings for about 15 to 20 minutes and I pray scriptures while doing it. This keeps my heart and body healthy, but doesn't take from the other areas or my time from others.

YOUR PERSONAL NEEDS
SCRIPTURES

*N*o temptation has seized you except what is common to man. And God is faithful; he will not let you be tempted beyond what you can bear. But when you are tempted, he will also provide a way out so that you can stand up under it.

1 Corinthians 10:13

Blessed is the man who perseveres under trial, because when he has stood the test, he will receive the crown of life that God has promised to those who love him.

James 1:12

Watch and pray so that you will not fall into temptation. The spirit is willing, but the body is weak.

Matthew 26:41

And lead us not into temptation, but deliver us from the evil one.

Matthew 6:13

Those on the rock are the ones who receive the word with joy when they hear it, but they have no root. They believe for a while, but in the time of testing they fall away.

Luke 8:13

On reaching the place, he said to them, "Pray that you will not fall into temptation."

"Why are you sleeping?" he asked them. "Get up and pray so that you will not fall into temptation."

Luke 22:40,46

If this is so, then the Lord knows how to rescue godly men from trials and to hold the unrighteous for the day of judgment, while continuing their punishment.

2 Peter 2:9

For this reason, when I could stand it no longer, I sent to find out about your faith. I was afraid that in some way the tempter might have tempted you and our efforts might have been useless.

1 Thessalonians 3:5

Because he himself suffered when he was tempted, he is able to help those who are being tempted.

Hebrews 2:18

For we do not have a high priest who is unable to sympathize with our weaknesses, but we have one who has been tempted in every way, just as we are – yet was without sin.

Hebrews 4:15

When tempted, no one should say, "God is tempting me." For God cannot be tempted by evil, nor does he tempt anyone;

But each one is tempted when, by his own evil desire, he is dragged away and enticed.

James 1:13,14

When You Feel Lonely

---

*B*ut if I do judge, my decisions are right, because I am not alone. I stand with the Father, who sent me.

The one who sent me is with me; he has not left me alone, for I always do what pleases him.

John 8:16,29

No one will be able to stand up against you all the days of your life. As I was with Moses, so I will be with you; I will never leave you nor forsake you.

Joshua 1:5

Keep your lives free from the love of money and be content with what you have, because God has said, "Never will I leave you; never will I forsake you."

Hebrews 13:5

And surely I am with you always, to the very end of the age.

Matthew 28:20b

The Lord replied, "My Presence will go with you, and I will give you rest."

Exodus 33:14

I will walk among you and be your God, and you will be my people.

Leviticus 26:12

For where two or three come together in my name, there am I with them.

Matthew 18:20

A man of many companions may come to ruin, but there is a friend who sticks closer than a brother.

Proverbs 18:24

When You Are Persecuted

---

*B*lessed are those who are persecuted because of righteousness, for theirs is the kingdom of heaven.

Blessed are you when people insult you, persecute you and falsely say all kinds of evil against you because of me.

Rejoice and be glad, because great is your reward in heaven, for in the same way they persecuted the prophets who were before you.

But I tell you: Love your enemies and pray for those who persecute you.

Matthew 5:10-12,44

Blessed are you when men hate you, when they exclude you and insult you and reject your name as evil, because of the Son of Man.

Luke 6:22

If the world hates you, keep in mind that it hated me first.

John 15:18

So do not be ashamed to testify about our Lord, or ashamed of me his prisoner. But join with me in suffering for the gospel, by the power of God.

2 Timothy 1:8

For which I am suffering even to the point of being chained like a criminal. But God's word is not chained.

Therefore I endure everything for the sake of the elect, that they too may obtain the salvation that is in Christ Jesus, with eternal glory.

Here is a trustworthy saying: If we died with him, we will also live with him;

If we endure, we will also reign with him. If we disown him, he will also disown us.

2 Timothy 2:9-12

Do not be surprised, my brothers, if the world hates you.

1 John 3:13

In fact, everyone who wants to live a godly life in Christ Jesus will be persecuted.

2 Timothy 3:12

Remember those earlier days after you had received the light, when you stood your ground in a great contest in the face of suffering.

Hebrews 10:32

He chose to be mistreated along with the people of God rather than to enjoy the pleasures of sin for a short time.

Hebrews 11:25

Consider him who endured such opposition from sinful men, so that you will not grow weary and lose heart.

Hebrews 12:3

But even if you should suffer for what is right, you are blessed. "Do not fear what they fear; do not be frightened."

Keeping a clear conscience, so that those who speak maliciously against your good behavior in Christ may be ashamed of their slander.

It is better, if it is God's will, to suffer for doing good than for doing evil.

1 Peter 3:14,16,17

For you have spent enough time in the past doing what pagans choose to do – living in debauchery, lust, drunkenness, orgies, carousing and detestable idolatry.

They think it strange that you do not plunge with them into the same flood of dissipation, and they heap abuse on you.

1 Peter 4:3,4

Dear friends, do not be surprised at the painful trial you are suffering, as though something strange were happening to you.

But rejoice that you participate in the sufferings of Christ, so that you may be overjoyed when his glory is revealed.

1 Peter 4:12,13

We had previously suffered and been insulted in Philippi, as you know, but with the help of our God we dared to tell you his gospel in spite of strong opposition.

1 Thessalonians 2:2

Therefore, among God's churches we boast about your perseverance and faith in all the persecutions and trials you are enduring.

2 Thessalonians 1:4

Now if we are children, then we are heirs – heirs of God and co-heirs with Christ, if indeed we share in his sufferings in order that we may also share in his glory.

Who shall separate us from the love of Christ? Shall trouble or hardship or persecution or famine or nakedness or danger or sword?

Romans 8:17,35

We are fools for Christ, but you are so wise in Christ! We are weak, but you are strong! You are honored, we are dishonored!

To this very hour we go hungry and thirsty, we are in rags, we are brutally treated, we are homeless.

We work hard with our own hands. When we are cursed, we bless; when we are persecuted, we endure it;

When we are slandered, we answer kindly. Up to this moment we have become the scum of the earth, the refuse of the world.

1 Corinthians 4:10-13

That is why, for Christ's sake, I delight in weaknesses, in insults, in hardships, in persecutions, in difficulties. For when I am weak, then I am strong.

2 Corinthians 12:10

Then they called them in again and commanded them not to speak or teach at all in the name of Jesus.

But Peter and John replied, "Judge for yourselves whether it is right in God's sight to obey you rather than God.

"For we cannot help speaking about what we have seen and heard."

Acts 4:18-20

Peter and the other apostles replied: "We must obey God rather than men!"

Acts 5:29

❧ *When You Feel Anxious or Worried* ❧

---

*D*o not be anxious about anything, but in everything, by prayer and petition, with thanksgiving, present your requests to God.

Philippians 4:6

Surely God is my salvation; I will trust and not be afraid. The Lord, the Lord, is my strength and my song; he has become my salvation.

Isaiah 12:2

And the peace of God, which transcends all understanding, will guard your hearts and your minds in Christ Jesus.

Philippians 4:7

Have I not commanded you? Be strong and courageous. Do not be terrified; do not be discouraged, for the Lord your God will be with you wherever you go.

Joshua 1:9

When you lie down, you will not be afraid; when you lie down, your sleep will be sweet.

Proverbs 3:24

Commit to the Lord whatever you do, and your plans will succeed.

Proverbs 16:3

Therefore I tell you, do not worry about your life, what you will eat or drink; or about your body, what you will wear. Is not life more important than food, and the body more important than clothes?

Matthew 6:25

So do not fear, for I am with you; do not be dismayed, for I am your God. I will strengthen you and help you; I will uphold you with my righteous right hand.

Isaiah 41:10

When You Want To   Be Close to God

---

*T*he Lord is good to those whose hope is in him, to the one who seeks him.

Lamentations 3:25

You will seek me and find me when you seek me with all your heart.

Jeremiah 29:13

Come near to God and he will come near to you. Wash your hands, you sinners, and purify your hearts, you double-minded.

James 4:8

But if from there you seek the Lord your God, you will find him if you look for him with all your heart and with all your soul.

Deuteronomy 4:29

He sought God during the days of Zechariah, who instructed him in the fear of God. As long as he sought the Lord, God gave him success.

2 Chronicles 26:5

One thing I ask of the Lord, this is what I seek: that I may dwell in the house of the Lord all the days of my life, to gaze upon the beauty of the Lord and to seek him in his temple.

For in the day of trouble he will keep me safe in his dwelling; he will hide me in the shelter of his tabernacle and set me high upon a rock.

Then my head will be exalted above the enemies who surround me; at his tabernacle will I sacrifice with shouts of joy; I will sing and make music to the Lord.

Hear my voice when I call, O Lord; be merciful to me and answer me.
My heart says of you, "Seek his face!" Your face, Lord, I will seek.

Psalm 27:4-8

As the deer pants for streams of water, so my soul pants for you, O God.
My soul thirsts for God, for the living God. When can I go and meet with God?

Psalm 42:1,2

O God, you are my God, earnestly I seek you; my soul thirsts for you, my body longs for you, in a dry and weary land where there is no water.
I have seen you in the sanctuary and beheld your power and your glory.

Psalm 63:1,2

The Lord is near to all who call on him, to all who call on him in truth.

Psalm 145:18

Blessed are those who hunger and thirst for righteousness, for they will be filled.

Matthew 5:6

God did this so that men would seek him and perhaps reach out for him and find him, though he is not far from each one of us.

Acts 17:27

The Spirit and the bride say, "Come!" And let him who hears say, "Come!"
Whoever is thirsty, let him come; and whoever wishes, let him take the free gift of the water of life.

Revelation 22:17

≈ *When You Fear Death* ≈

---

*S*ince the children have flesh and blood, he too shared in their humanity so that by his death he might destroy him who holds the power of death – that is, the devil –
And free those who all their lives were held in slavery by their fear of death.

Hebrews 2:14,15

But it has now been revealed through the appearing of our Savior, Christ Jesus, who has destroyed death and has brought life and immortality to light through the gospel.

2 Timothy 1:10

The last enemy to be destroyed is death.

"Where, O death, is your victory? Where, O death, is your sting?"

The sting of death is sin, and the power of sin is the law.

But thanks be to God! He gives us the victory through our Lord Jesus Christ.

1 Corinthians 15:26,55-57

When I saw him, I fell at his feet as though dead. Then he placed his right hand on me and said: "Do not be afraid. I am the First and the Last.

"I am the Living One; I was dead, and behold I am alive for ever and ever! And I hold the keys of death and Hades."

Revelation 1:17,18

If we live, we live to the Lord; and if we die, we die to the Lord. So, whether we live or die, we belong to the Lord.

Romans 14:8

For to me, to live is Christ and to die is gain.

Philippians 1:21

Even though I walk through the valley of the shadow of death, I will fear no evil, for you are with me; your rod and your staff, they comfort me.

Psalm 23:4

When calamity comes, the wicked are brought down, but even in death the righteous have a refuge.

Proverbs 14:32

Who shall separate us from the love of Christ? Shall trouble or hardship or persecution or famine or nakedness or danger or sword?

Romans 8:35

Now we know that if the earthly tent we live in is destroyed, we have a building from God, an eternal house in heaven, not built by human hands.

2 Corinthians 5:1

Do not let your hearts be troubled. Trust in God; trust also in me.

John 14:1

With long life will I satisfy him and show him my salvation.

Psalm 91:16

≈ *When You Feel Afraid* ≈

*E*ven though I walk through the valley of the shadow of death, I will fear no evil, for you are with me; your rod and your staff, they comfort me.

Psalm 23:4

The Lord is my light and my salvation – whom shall I fear? The Lord is the stronghold of my life – of whom shall I be afraid?

Psalm 27:1

In God, whose word I praise, in God I trust; I will not be afraid. What can mortal man do to me?

Psalm 56:4

The Lord is with me; I will not be afraid. What can man do to me?

Psalm 118:6

You will not fear the terror of night, nor the arrow that flies by day.
Then no harm will befall you, no disaster will come near your tent.

Psalm 91:5,10

I will not fear the tens of thousands drawn up against me on every side.

Psalm 3:6

So do not fear, for I am with you; do not be dismayed, for I am your God, I will strengthen you and help you; I will uphold you with my righteous right hand.
For I am the Lord, your God, who takes hold of your right hand and says to you, Do not fear; I will help you.

Isaiah 41:10,13

But now, this is what the Lord says – he who created you, O Jacob, he who formed you, O Israel: "Fear not, for I have redeemed you; I have summoned you by name; you are mine."

Isaiah 43:1

Do not be afraid, for I am with you; I will bring your children from the east and gather you from the west.

Isaiah 43:5

Do not tremble, do not be afraid. Did I not proclaim this and foretell it long ago? You are my witnesses. Is there any God besides me? No, there is no other Rock; I know not one.

Isaiah 44:8

So do not be afraid of them. There is nothing concealed that will not be disclosed, or hidden that will not be made known.

Matthew 10:26

Because of my chains, most of the brothers in the Lord have been encouraged to speak the word of God more courageously and fearlessly.

Philippians 1:14

For God did not give us a spirit of timidity, but a spirit of power, of love and of self-discipline.

2 Timothy 1:7

So we say with confidence, "The Lord is my helper; I will not be afraid. What can man do to me?"

Hebrews 13:6

There is no fear in love. But perfect love drives out fear, because fear has to do with punishment. The one who fears is not made perfect in love.

1 John 4:18

When You Feel Frustrated

---

*S*o he said to me, "This is the word of the Lord to Zerubbabel: 'Not by might nor by power, but by my Spirit,' says the Lord Almighty."

Zechariah 4:6

Peace I leave with you; my peace I give you. I do not give to you as the world gives. Do not let your hearts be troubled and do not be afraid.

John 14:27

There remains, then, a Sabbath-rest for the people of God; for anyone who enters God's rest also rests from his own work, just as God did from his.

Let us, therefore, make every effort to enter that rest, so that no one will fall by following their example of disobedience.

For the word of God is living and active. Sharper than any double-edged sword, it penetrates even to dividing soul and spirit, joints and marrow; it judges the thoughts and attitudes of the heart.

Let us then approach the throne of grace with confidence, so that we may receive mercy and find grace to help us in our time of need.

Hebrews 4:9-12,16

Therefore let everyone who is godly pray to you while you may be found; surely when the mighty waters rise, they will not reach him.

You are my hiding place; you will protect me from trouble and surround me with songs of deliverance. *Selah*

I will instruct you and teach you in the way you should go; I will counsel you and watch over you.

Do not be like the horse or the mule, which have no understanding but must be controlled by bit and bridle or they will not come to you.

Many are the woes of the wicked, but the Lord's unfailing love surrounds the man who trusts in him.

Rejoice in the Lord and be glad, you righteous; sing, all you who are upright in heart!

Psalm 32:6-11

The path of the righteous is like the first gleam of dawn, shining ever brighter till the full light of day.

Proverbs 4:18

Commit to the Lord whatever you do, and your plans will succeed.

Proverbs 16:3

I am still confident of this: I will see the goodness of the Lord in the land of the living.

Wait for the Lord; be strong and take heart and wait for the Lord.

Psalm 27:13,14

My flesh and my heart may fail, but God is the strength of my heart and my portion forever.

Those who are far from you will perish; you destroy all who are unfaithful to you.

But as for me, it is good to be near God. I have made the Sovereign Lord my refuge; I will tell of all your deeds.

Psalm 73:26-28

You will keep in perfect peace him whose mind is steadfast, because he trusts in you.

Trust in the Lord forever, for the Lord, the Lord, is the Rock eternal.

Isaiah 26:3,4

Let us therefore make every effort to do what leads to peace and to mutual edification.

Romans 14:19

Let the peace of Christ rule in your hearts, since as members of one body you were called to peace. And be thankful.

Colossians 3:15

To the Jews who had believed him, Jesus said, "If you hold to my teaching, you are really my disciples.

"Then you will know the truth, and the truth will set you free."

John 8:31,32

≈ *When You Need Guidance From God* ≈

---

*L*ead me, O Lord, in your righteousness because of my enemies – make straight your way before me.

Psalm 5:8

In you I trust, O my God. Do not let me be put to shame, nor let my enemies triumph over me.

Psalm 25:2

He guides the humble in what is right and teaches them his way.

Psalm 25:9

Teach me your way, O Lord; lead me in a straight path because of my oppressors.

Psalm 27:11

I will instruct you and teach you in the way you should go; I will counsel you and watch over you.

Psalm 32:8

Since you are my rock and my fortress, for the sake of your name lead and guide me.

Psalm 31:3

For this God is our God for ever and ever; he will be our guide even to the end.

Psalm 48:14

You guide me with your counsel, and afterward you will take me into glory.

Psalm 73:24

I will lead the blind by ways they have not known, along unfamiliar paths I will guide them; I will turn the darkness into light before them and make the rough places smooth. These are the things I will do; I will not forsake them.

Isaiah 42:16

This is what the Lord says – your Redeemer, the Holy One of Israel: "I am the Lord your God, who teaches you what is best for you, who directs you in the way you should go."

Isaiah 48:17

The Lord will guide you always; he will satisfy your needs in a sun-scorched land and will strengthen your frame. You will be like a well-watered garden, like a spring whose waters never fail.

Isaiah 58:11

To shine on those living in darkness and in the shadow of death, to guide our feet into the path of peace.

Luke 1:79

The watchman opens the gate for him, and the sheep listen to his voice. He calls his own sheep by name and leads them out.

John 10:3

You have made known to me the path of life; you will fill me with joy in your presence, with eternal pleasures at your right hand.

Psalm 16:11

But when he, the Spirit of truth, comes, he will guide you into all truth. He will not speak on his own; he will speak only what he hears, and he will tell you what is yet to come.

John 16:13

Direct me in the path of your commands, for there I find delight.

Psalm 119:35

Your word is a lamp to my feet and a light for my path.

Psalm 119:105

Direct my footsteps according to your word; let no sin rule over me.

Psalm 119:133

If the Lord delights in a man's way, he makes his steps firm.

Psalm 37:23

Then the Lord replied: "Write down the revelation and make it plain on tablets so that a herald may run with it.

"For the revelation awaits an appointed time; it speaks of the end and will not prove false. Though it linger, wait for it; it will certainly come and will not delay."

Habakkuk 2:2,3

Where there is no revelation, the people cast off restraint; but blessed is he who keeps the law.

Proverbs 29:18

In the last days, God says, I will pour out my Spirit on all people. Your sons and daughters will prophesy, your young men will see visions, your old men will dream dreams.

Acts 2:17

In him we were also chosen, having been predestined according to the plan of him who works out everything in conformity with the purpose of his will.

Ephesians 1:11

In his heart a man plans his course, but the Lord determines his steps.

Proverbs 16:9

Do you not know that in a race all the runners run, but only one gets the prize? Run in such a way as to get the prize.

Everyone who competes in the games goes into strict training. They do it to get a crown that will not last; but we do it to get a crown that will last forever.

Therefore I do not run like a man running aimlessly; I do not fight like a man beating the air.

1 Corinthians 9:24-26

When You Want To Be a Witness for Christ

*Y*ou are the light of the world. A city on a hill cannot be hidden.

In the same way, let your light shine before men, that they may see your good deeds and praise your Father in heaven.

Matthew 5:14,16

For Christ did not send me to baptize, but to preach the gospel – not with words of human wisdom, lest the cross of Christ be emptied of its power.

For the message of the cross is foolishness to those who are perishing, but to us who are being saved it is the power of God.

For it is written: "I will destroy the wisdom of the wise; the intelligence of the intelligent I will frustrate."

Where is the wise man? Where is the scholar? Where is the philosopher of this age? Has not God made foolish the wisdom of the world?

For since in the wisdom of God the world through its wisdom did not know him, God was pleased through the foolishness of what was preached to save those who believe.

Jews demand miraculous signs and Greeks look for wisdom,

But we preach Christ crucified: a stumbling block to Jews and foolishness to Gentiles,

But to those whom God has called, both Jews and Greeks, Christ the power of God and the wisdom of God.

For the foolishness of God is wiser than man's wisdom, and the weakness of God is stronger than man's strength.

Brothers, think of what you were when you were called. Not many of you were wise by human standards; not many were influential; not many were of noble birth.

But God chose the foolish things of the world to shame the wise; God chose the weak things of the world to shame the strong.

He chose the lowly things of this world and the despised things – and the things that are not – to nullify the things that are,

So that no one may boast before him.

1 Corinthians 1:17-29

When I came to you, brothers, I did not come with eloquence or superior wisdom as I proclaimed to you the testimony about God.

For I resolved to know nothing while I was with you except Jesus Christ and him crucified.

I came to you in weakness and fear, and with much trembling.

My message and my preaching were not with wise and persuasive words, but with a demonstration of the Spirit's power,

So that your faith might not rest on men's wisdom, but on God's power.

1 Corinthians 2:1-5

But thanks be to God, who always leads us in triumphal procession in Christ and through us spreads everywhere the fragrance of the knowledge of him.

For we are to God the aroma of Christ among those who are being saved and those who are perishing.

To the one we are the smell of death; to the other, the fragrance of life. And who is equal to such a task?

2 Corinthians 2:14-16

To them God has chosen to make known among the Gentiles the glorious riches of this mystery, which is Christ in you, the hope of glory.

We proclaim him, admonishing and teaching everyone with all wisdom, so that we may present everyone perfect in Christ.

To this end I labor, struggling with all his energy, which so powerfully works in me.

Colossians 1:27-29

Do your best to present yourself to God as one approved, a workman who does not need to be ashamed and who correctly handles the word of truth.

2 Timothy 2:15

So that you may become blameless and pure, children of God without fault in a crooked and depraved generation, in which you shine like stars in the universe.

Philippians 2:15

And teaching them to obey everything I have commanded you. And surely I am with you always, to the very end of the age.

Matthew 28:20

By this all men will know that you are my disciples, if you love one another.

John 13:35

But you are a chosen people, a royal priesthood, a holy nation, a people belonging to God, that you may declare the praises of him who called you out of darkness into his wonderful light.

1 Peter 2:9

And this gospel of the kingdom will be preached in the whole world as a testimony to all nations, and then the end will come.

Matthew 24:14

The Spirit of the Sovereign Lord is on me, because the Lord has anointed me to preach good news to the poor. He has sent me to bind up the brokenhearted, to proclaim freedom for the captives and release from darkness for the prisoners.

Isaiah 61:1

Pray also for me, that whenever I open my mouth, words may be given me so that I will fearlessly make known the mystery of the gospel.

Ephesians 6:19

The Spirit of the Lord is on me, because he has anointed me to preach good news to the poor. He has sent me to proclaim freedom for the prisoners and recovery of sight for the blind, to release the oppressed.

Luke 4:18

All this is from God, who reconciled us to himself through Christ and gave us the ministry of reconciliation:

That God was reconciling the world to himself in Christ, not counting men's sins against them. And he has committed to us the message of reconciliation.

We are therefore Christ's ambassadors, as though God were making his appeal through us. We implore you on Christ's behalf: Be reconciled to God.

2 Corinthians 5:18-20

≈ *When You Need Peace* ≈

I will grant peace in the land, and you will lie down and no one will make you afraid. I will remove savage beasts from the land, and the sword will not pass through your country.

Leviticus 26:6

You will keep in perfect peace him whose mind is steadfast, because he trusts in you.

Isaiah 26:3

I will lie down and sleep in peace, for you alone, O Lord, make me dwell in safety.

Psalm 4:8

The Lord gives strength to his people; the Lord blesses his people with peace.

Psalm 29:11

Whom have I in heaven but you? And earth has nothing I desire besides you. My flesh and my heart may fail, but God is the strength of my heart and my portion forever.

Psalm 73:25,26

Now may the Lord of peace himself give you peace at all times in every way. The Lord be with all of you.

2 Thessalonians 3:16

Great peace have they who love your law, and nothing can make them stumble.

Psalm 119:165

I will listen to what God the Lord will say; he promises peace to his people, his saints – but let them not return to folly.

Psalm 85:8

I will heal my people and will let them enjoy abundant peace and security.

Jeremiah 33:6b

Glory to God in the highest, and on earth peace to men on whom his favor rests.

Luke 2:14

On the evening of that first day of the week, when the disciples were together, with the doors locked for fear of the Jews, Jesus came and stood among them and said, "Peace be with you!"

John 20:19

Peace I leave with you; my peace I give you. I do not give to you as the world gives. Do not let your hearts be troubled and do not be afraid.

John 14:27

Therefore, since we have been justified through faith, we have peace with God through our Lord Jesus Christ.

Romans 5:1

For the kingdom of God is not a matter of eating and drinking, but of righteousness, peace and joy in the Holy Spirit.

Romans 14:17

May the God of hope fill you with all joy and peace as you trust in him, so that you may overflow with hope by the power of the Holy Spirit.

Romans 15:13

Do not be anxious about anything, but in everything, by prayer and petition, with thanksgiving, present your requests to God.
And the peace of God, which transcends all understanding, will guard your hearts and your minds in Christ Jesus.

Philippians 4:6,7

Let the peace of Christ rule in your hearts, since as members of one body you were called to peace. And be thankful.

Colossians 3:15

I have told you these things, so that in me you may have peace. In this world you will have trouble. But take heart! I have overcome the world.

John 16:33

 ## *When You Need Forgiveness*

---

ut with you there is forgiveness; therefore you are feared.

Psalm 130:4

Blessed is he whose transgressions are forgiven, whose sins are covered.

Psalm 32:1

Therefore, my brothers, I want you to know that through Jesus the forgiveness of sins is proclaimed to you.

Acts 13:38

To open their eyes and turn them from darkness to light, and from the power of Satan to God, so that they may receive forgiveness of sins and a place among those who are sanctified by faith in me.

Acts 26:18

In him we have redemption through his blood, the forgiveness of sins, in accordance with the riches of God's grace.

Ephesians 1:7

Look upon my affliction and my distress and take away all my sins.

Psalm 25:18

You are forgiving and good, O Lord, abounding in love to all who call to you.

Psalm 86:5

"No longer will a man teach his neighbor, or a man his brother, saying, 'Know the Lord,' because they will all know me, from the least of them to the greatest," declares the Lord. "For I will forgive their wickedness and will remember their sins no more."

Jeremiah 31:34

For if you forgive men when they sin against you, your heavenly Father will also forgive you.

But if you do not forgive men their sins, your Father will not forgive your sins.

Matthew 6:14,15

And when you stand praying, if you hold anything against anyone, forgive him, so that your Father in heaven may forgive you your sins.

Mark 11:25

So watch yourselves. "If your brother sins, rebuke him, and if he repents, forgive him.

"If he sins against you seven times in a day, and seven times comes back to you and says, 'I repent,' forgive him."

Luke 17:3,4

Jesus said, "Father, forgive them, for they do not know what they are doing."

Luke 23:34a

When you were dead in your sins and in the uncircumcision of your sinful nature, God made you alive with Christ. He forgave us all our sins.

Colossians 2:13

❧ *When You Need Healing* ❧

---

*S*urely he took up our infirmities and carried our sorrows, yet we considered him stricken by God, smitten by him, and afflicted.

But he was pierced for our transgressions, he was crushed for our iniquities; the punishment that brought us peace was upon him, and by his wounds we are healed.

Isaiah 53:4,5

Praise the Lord, O my soul, and forget not all his benefits –
Who forgives all your sins and heals all your diseases.

Psalm 103:2,3

He said, "If you listen carefully to the voice of the Lord your God and do what is right in his eyes, if you pay attention to his commands and keep all his decrees, I will not bring on you any of the diseases I brought on the Egyptians, for I am the Lord, who heals you."

Exodus 15:26

Jesus went throughout Galilee, teaching in their synagogues, preaching the good news of the kingdom, and healing every disease and sickness among the people.

Matthew 4:23

But for you who revere my name, the sun of righteousness will rise with healing in its wings. And you will go out and leap like calves released from the stall.

Malachi 4:2

How God anointed Jesus of Nazareth with the Holy Spirit and power, and how he went around doing good and healing all who were under the power of the devil, because God was with him.

Acts 10:38

The Spirit of the Lord is on me, because he has anointed me to preach good news to the poor. He has sent me to proclaim freedom for the prisoners and recovery of sight for the blind, to release the oppressed.

Luke 4:18

He sent forth his word and healed them; he rescued them from the grave.

Psalm 107:20

The centurion replied, "Lord, I do not deserve to have you come under my roof. But just say the word, and my servant will be healed.

"For I myself am a man under authority, with soldiers under me. I tell this one, 'Go,' and he goes; and that one, 'Come,' and he comes. I say to my servant, 'Do this,' and he does it."

When Jesus heard this, he was astonished and said to those following him, "I tell you the truth, I have not found anyone in Israel with such great faith.

"I say to you that many will come from the east and the west, and will take their places at the feast with Abraham, Isaac and Jacob in the kingdom of heaven.

"But the subjects of the kingdom will be thrown outside, into the darkness, where there will be weeping and gnashing of teeth."

Then Jesus said to the centurion, "Go! It will be done just as you believed it would." And his servant was healed at that very hour.

When Jesus came into Peter's house, he saw Peter's mother-in-law lying in bed with a fever.

He touched her hand and the fever left her, and she got up and began to wait on him.

When evening came, many who were demon-possessed were brought to him, and he drove out the spirits with a word and healed all the sick.

Matthew 8:8-16

For they [God's words] are life to those who find them and health to a man's whole body.

Proverbs 4:22

A cheerful heart is good medicine, but a crushed spirit dries up the bones.

Proverbs 17:22

Dear friend, I pray that you may enjoy good health and that all may go well with you, even as your soul is getting along well.

3 John 2

When Jesus landed and saw a large crowd, he had compassion on them and healed their sick.

Matthew 14:14

Therefore confess your sins to each other and pray for each other so that you may be healed. The prayer of a righteous man is powerful and effective.

James 5:16

He himself bore our sins in his body on the tree, so that we might die to sins and live for righteousness; by his wounds you have been healed.

1 Peter 2:24

And these signs will accompany those who believe: In my name they will drive out demons; they will speak in new tongues;

They will pick up snakes with their hands; and when they drink deadly poison, it will not hurt them at all; they will place their hands on sick people, and they will get well.

Mark 16:17,18

When You Need Wisdom

---

*G*od gave Solomon wisdom and very great insight, and a breadth of understanding as measureless as the sand on the seashore.

Solomon's wisdom was greater than the wisdom of all the men of the East, and greater than all the wisdom of Egypt.

He was wiser than any other man, including Ethan the Ezrahite – wiser than Heman, Calcol and Darda, the sons of Mahol. And his fame spread to all the surrounding nations.

He spoke three thousand proverbs and his songs numbered a thousand and five.

He described plant life, from the cedar of Lebanon to the hyssop that grows out of walls. He also taught about animals and birds, reptiles and fish.

Men of all nations came to listen to Solomon's wisdom, sent by all the kings of the world, who had heard of his wisdom.

1 Kings 4:29-34

The Lord gave Solomon wisdom, just as he had promised him. There were peaceful relations between Hiram and Solomon, and the two of them made a treaty.

1 Kings 5:12

May the Lord give you discretion and understanding when he puts you in command over Israel, so that you may keep the law of the Lord your God.

1 Chronicles 22:12

Surely you desire truth in the inner parts; you teach me wisdom in the inmost place.

Psalm 51:6

Teach us to number our days aright, that we may gain a heart of wisdom.

Psalm 90:12

The fear of the Lord is the beginning of wisdom; all who follow his precepts have good understanding. To him belongs eternal praise.

Psalm 111:10

Turning your ear to wisdom and applying your heart to understanding,
And if you call out for insight and cry aloud for understanding,
And if you look for it as for silver and search for it as for hidden treasure,
Then you will understand the fear of the Lord and find the knowledge of God.
For the Lord gives wisdom, and from his mouth come knowledge and understanding.
He holds victory in store for the upright, he is a shield to those whose walk is blameless.

Proverbs 2:2-7

Blessed is the man who finds wisdom, the man who gains understanding.

Proverbs 3:13

Wisdom is supreme; therefore get wisdom. Though it cost all you have, get understanding.
I guide you in the way of wisdom and lead you along straight paths.

Proverbs 4:7,11

For wisdom is more precious than rubies, and nothing you desire can compare with her.
I, wisdom, dwell together with prudence; I possess knowledge and discretion.

Proverbs 8:11,12

How much better to get wisdom than gold, to choose understanding rather than silver!

Proverbs 16:16

He who gets wisdom loves his own soul; he who cherishes understanding prospers.

Proverbs 19:8

And the child grew and became strong; he was filled with wisdom, and the grace of God was upon him.

Luke 2:40

But to those whom God has called, both Jews and Greeks, Christ the power of God and the wisdom of God.

For the foolishness of God is wiser than man's wisdom, and the weakness of God is stronger than man's strength.

1 Corinthians 1:24,25

We do, however, speak a message of wisdom among the mature, but not the wisdom of this age or of the rulers of this age, who are coming to nothing.

1 Corinthians 2:6

For the wisdom of this world is foolishness in God's sight. As it is written: "He catches the wise in their craftiness."

1 Corinthians 3:19

That he lavished on us with all wisdom and understanding.

I keep asking that the God of our Lord Jesus Christ, the glorious Father, may give you the Spirit of wisdom and revelation, so that you may know him better.

Ephesians 1:8,17

For this reason, since the day we heard about you, we have not stopped praying for you and asking God to fill you with the knowledge of his will through all spiritual wisdom and understanding.

Colossians 1:9

Let the word of Christ dwell in you richly as you teach and admonish one another with all wisdom, and as you sing psalms, hymns and spiritual songs with gratitude in your hearts to God.

Colossians 3:16

If any of you lacks wisdom, he should ask God, who gives generously to all without finding fault, and it will be given to him.

James 1:5

≋ *When You Need Joy* ≋

---

or his anger lasts only a moment, but his favor lasts a lifetime; weeping may remain for a night, but rejoicing comes in the morning.

Psalm 30:5

Rejoice in the Lord and be glad, you righteous; sing, all you who are upright in heart!

Psalm 32:11

But may all who seek you rejoice and be glad in you; may those who love your salvation always say, "The Lord be exalted!"

Psalm 40:16

Let me hear joy and gladness; let the bones you have crushed rejoice.

Psalm 51:8

Shout for joy to the Lord, all the earth.
Worship the Lord with gladness; come before him with joyful songs.

Psalm 100:1,2

Those who sow in tears will reap with songs of joy.
He who goes out weeping, carrying seed to sow, will return with songs of joy, carrying sheaves with him.

Psalm 126:5,6

Nehemiah said, "Go and enjoy choice food and sweet drinks, and send some to those who have nothing prepared. This day is sacred to our Lord. Do not grieve, for the joy of the Lord is your strength."

Nehemiah 8:10

Be joyful always.

1 Thessalonians 5:16

Consider it pure joy, my brothers, whenever you face trials of many kinds.

James 1:2

Is any one of you in trouble? He should pray. Is anyone happy? Let him sing songs of praise.

James 5:13

I have told you this so that my joy may be in you and that your joy may be complete.

John 15:11

Until now you have not asked for anything in my name. Ask and you will receive, and your joy will be complete.

I have told you these things, so that in me you may have peace. In this world you will have trouble. But take heart! I have overcome the world.

John 16:24,33

I am coming to you now, but I say these things while I am still in the world, so that they may have the full measure of my joy within them.

John 17:13

You have made known to me the paths of life; you will fill me with joy in your presence.

Acts 2:28

For the kingdom of God is not a matter of eating and drinking, but of righteousness, peace and joy in the Holy Spirit.

Romans 14:17

May the God of hope fill you with all joy and peace as you trust in him, so that you may overflow with hope by the power of the Holy Spirit.

Romans 15:13

But the fruit of the Spirit is love, joy, peace, patience, kindness, goodness, faithfulness, gentleness and self-control.

Galatians 5:22,23

Rejoice in the Lord always. I will say it again: Rejoice!

Philippians 4:4

Though you have not seen him, you love him; and even though you do not see him now, you believe in him and are filled with an inexpressible and glorious joy.

1 Peter 1:8

❧ *When You Need Self-Control* ❧

*P*ut to death, therefore, whatever belongs to your earthly nature: sexual immorality, impurity, lust, evil desires and greed, which is idolatry.

Colossians 3:5

Rather, clothe yourselves with the Lord Jesus Christ, and do not think about how to gratify the desires of the sinful nature.

Romans 13:14

Everyone who competes in the games goes into strict training. They do it to get a crown that will not last; but we do it to get a crown that will last forever.

1 Corinthians 9:25

Let your gentleness be evident to all. The Lord is near.

Philippians 4:5

So I say, live by the Spirit, and you will not gratify the desires of the sinful nature.

Galatians 5:16

"Everything is permissible for me" – but not everything is beneficial. "Everything is permissible for me" – but I will not be mastered by anything.

1 Corinthians 6:12

"Everything is permissible" – but not everything is beneficial. "Everything is permissible" – but not everything is constructive.

1 Corinthians 10:23

I have been crucified with Christ and I no longer live, but Christ lives in me. The life I live in the body, I live by faith in the Son of God, who loved me and gave himself for me.

Galatians 2:20

(The grace of God) teaches us to say "No" to ungodliness and worldly passions, and to live self-controlled, upright and godly lives in this present age.

Titus 2:12

For this very reason, make every effort to add to your faith goodness; and to goodness, knowledge;

And to knowledge, self-control; and to self-control, perseverance; and to perseverance, godliness.

2 Peter 1:5,6

Better a patient man than a warrior, a man who controls his temper than one who takes a city.

Proverbs 16:32

❧ *When You Need Favor* ❧

---

*N*o one will be able to stand up against you all the days of your life. As I was with Moses, so I will be with you; I will never leave you nor forsake you.

Joshua 1:5

For surely, O Lord, you bless the righteous; you surround them with your favor as with a shield.

Psalm 5:12

Then you will win favor and a good name in the sight of God and man.

Proverbs 3:4

For whoever finds me finds life and receives favor from the Lord.

Proverbs 8:35

A good man obtains favor from the Lord, but the Lord condemns a crafty man.

Proverbs 12:2

Fools mock at making amends for sin, but goodwill is found among the upright.

Proverbs 14:9

The angel went to her and said, "Greetings, you who are highly favored! The Lord is with you."

Mary was greatly troubled at his words and wondered what kind of greeting this might be.

But the angel said to her, "Do not be afraid, Mary, you have found favor with God."

Luke 1:28-30

Let us then approach the throne of grace with confidence, so that we may receive mercy and find grace to help us in our time of need.

Hebrews 4:16

But you are a chosen people, a royal priesthood, a holy nation, a people belonging to God, that you may declare the praises of him who called you out of darkness into his wonderful light.

1 Peter 2:9

Mordecai had a cousin named Hadassah, whom he had brought up because she had neither father nor mother. This girl, who was also known as Esther, was lovely in form and features, and Mordecai had taken her as his own daughter when her father and mother died.

When the turn came for Esther (the girl Mordecai had adopted, the daughter of his uncle Abihail) to go to the king, she asked for nothing other than what Hegai, the king's eunuch who was in charge of the harem, suggested. And Esther won the favor of everyone who saw her.

Esther 2:7,15

When he saw Queen Esther standing in the court, he was pleased with her and held out to her the gold scepter that was in his hand. So Esther approached and touched the tip of the scepter.

Esther 5:2

Then Queen Esther answered, "If I have found favor with you, O king, and if it pleases your majesty, grant me my life – this is my petition. And spare my people – this is my request."

Esther 7:3

"If it pleases the king," she said, "and if he regards me with favor and thinks it the right thing to do, and if he is pleased with me, let an order be written overruling the dispatches that Haman son of Hammedatha, the Agagite, devised and wrote to destroy the Jews in all the king's provinces."

Esther 8:5

❧ *When you Need Comfort* ❧

---

*T*he eternal God is your refuge, and underneath are the everlasting arms. He will drive out your enemy before you, saying, "Destroy him!"

Deuteronomy 33:27

Even though I walk through the valley of the shadow of death, I will fear no evil, for you are with me; your rod and your staff, they comfort me.

Psalm 23:4

For in the day of trouble he will keep me safe in his dwelling; he will hide me in the shelter of his tabernacle and set me high upon a rock.

Psalm 27:5

For his anger lasts only a moment, but his favor lasts a lifetime; weeping may remain for a night, but rejoicing comes in the morning.

Psalm 30:5

I will extol the Lord at all times; his praise will always be on my lips.
My soul will boast in the Lord; let the afflicted hear and rejoice.
Glorify the Lord with me; let us exalt his name together.
I sought the Lord, and he answered me; he delivered me from all my fears.
Those who look to him are radiant; their faces are never covered with shame.
This poor man called, and the Lord heard him; he saved him out of all his troubles.
The angel of the Lord encamps around those who fear him, and he delivers them.
Taste and see that the Lord is good; blessed is the man who takes refuge in him.
Fear the Lord, you his saints, for those who fear him lack nothing.

Psalm 34:1-9

God is our refuge and strength, an ever-present help in trouble.

Psalm 46:1

And call upon me in the day of trouble; I will deliver you, and you will honor me.

Psalm 50:15

Cast your cares on the Lord and he will sustain you; he will never let the righteous fall.

Psalm 55:22

Even in the darkness light dawns for the upright, for the gracious and compassionate and righteous man.

Psalm 112:4

Praise be to the God and Father of our Lord Jesus Christ, the Father of compassion and the God of all comfort,

Who comforts us in all our troubles, so that we can comfort those in any trouble with the comfort we ourselves have received from God.

2 Corinthians 1:3,4

We are hard pressed on every side, but not crushed; perplexed, but not in despair;

Persecuted, but not abandoned; struck down, but not destroyed.

2 Corinthians 4:8,9

He heals the brokenhearted and binds up their wounds.

Psalm 147:3

So do not fear, for I am with you; do not be dismayed, for I am your God. I will strengthen you and help you; I will uphold you with my righteous right hand.

Isaiah 41:10

When you pass through the waters, I will be with you; and when you pass through the rivers, they will not sweep over you. When you walk through the fire, you will not be burned; the flames will not set you ablaze.

Isaiah 43:2

The Lord is good, a refuge in times of trouble. He cares for those who trust in him.

Nahum 1:7

Blessed are those who mourn, for they will be comforted.

Matthew 5:4

Come to me, all you who are weary and burdened, and I will give you rest.

Matthew 11:28

Do not let your hearts be troubled. Trust in God; trust also in me.

And I will ask the Father, and he will give you another Counselor to be with you forever –

I will not leave you as orphans; I will come to you.

John 14:1,16,18

Peace I leave with you; my peace I give you. I do not give to you as the world gives. Do not let your hearts be troubled and do not be afraid.

John 14:27

And we know that in all things God works for the good of those who love him, who have been called according to his purpose.

Who shall separate us from the love of Christ? Shall trouble or hardship or persecution or famine or nakedness or danger or sword?

Romans 8:28,35

Carry each other's burdens, and in this way you will fulfill the law of Christ.

Galatians 6:2

✑ *When You Need Strength* ✑

---

*B*eat your plowshares into swords and your pruning hooks into spears. Let the weakling say, "I am strong!"

Joel 3:10

Finally, be strong in the Lord and in his mighty power.

Ephesians 6:10

Be on your guard; stand firm in the faith; be men of courage; be strong.

1 Corinthians 16:13

You then, my son, be strong in the grace that is in Christ Jesus.

2 Timothy 2:1

What, then, shall we say in response to this? If God is for us, who can be against us?

He who did not spare his own Son, but gave him up for us all – how will he not also, along with him, graciously give us all things?

Romans 8:31,32

I pray that out of his glorious riches he may strengthen you with power through his Spirit in your inner being.

Ephesians 3:16

Being strengthened with all power according to his glorious might so that you may have great endurance and patience, and joyfully

Giving thanks to the Father, who has qualified you to share in the inheritance of the saints in the kingdom of light.

Colossians 1:11,12

But the Lord stood at my side and gave me strength, so that through me the message might be fully proclaimed and all the Gentiles might hear it. And I was delivered from the lion's mouth.

2 Timothy 4:17

I can do everything through him who gives me strength.

Philippians 4:13

You see, at just the right time, when we were still powerless, Christ died for the ungodly.

Romans 5:6

The Sovereign Lord is my strength.

Habakkuk 3:19a

Yet he did not waver through unbelief regarding the promise of God, but was strengthened in his faith and gave glory to God.

Romans 4:20

When You Need Protection

---

*H*e who dwells in the shelter of the Most High will rest in the shadow of the Almighty.

I will say of the Lord, "He is my refuge and my fortress, my God, in whom I trust."

Surely he will save you from the fowler's snare and from the deadly pestilence.

A thousand may fall at your side, ten thousand at your right hand, but it will not come near you.

Then no harm will befall you, no disaster will come near your tent.

"Because he loves me," says the Lord, "I will rescue him; I will protect him, for he acknowledges my name.

"He will call upon me, and I will answer him; I will be with him in trouble, I will deliver him and honor him."

Psalm 91:1-3,7,10,14,15

The angel of the Lord encamps around those who fear him, and he delivers them.

Psalm 34:7

You are my hiding place; you will protect me from trouble and surround me with songs of deliverance. *Selah*

Psalm 32:7

Even though I walk through the valley of the shadow of death, I will fear no evil, for you are with me; your rod and your staff, they comfort me.

Psalm 23:4

But not a hair of your head will perish.

Luke 21:18

He said: "Listen, King Jehoshaphat and all who live in Judah and Jerusalem! This is what the Lord says to you: 'Do not be afraid or discouraged because of this vast army. For the battle is not yours, but God's.

"'You will not have to fight this battle. Take up your positions; stand firm and see the deliverance the Lord will give you, O Judah and Jerusalem. Do not be afraid; do not be discouraged. Go out to face them tomorrow, and the Lord will be with you.'"

2 Chronicles 20:15,17

As the mountains surround Jerusalem, so the Lord surrounds his people both now and forevermore.

Psalm 125:2

Have you not put a hedge around him and his household and everything he has? You have blessed the work of his hands, so that his flocks and herds are spread throughout the land.

Job 1:10

The Lord your God, who is going before you, will fight for you, as he did for you in Egypt, before your very eyes.

Deuteronomy 1:30

You alone are the Lord. You made the heavens, even the highest heavens, and all their starry host, the earth and all that is on it, the seas and all that is in them. You give life to everything, and the multitudes of heaven worship you.

Nehemiah 9:6

He rescued me from my powerful enemy, from my foes, who were too strong for me.

Psalm 18:17

For you have been my refuge, a strong tower against the foe.

Psalm 61:3

When you lie down, you will not be afraid; when you lie down, your sleep will be sweet.

Proverbs 3:24

When you pass through the waters, I will be with you; and when you pass through the rivers, they will not sweep over you. When you walk through the fire, you will not be burned; the flames will not set you ablaze.

Isaiah 43:2

≈ *When You Need Faith* ≈

I tell you the truth, if anyone says to this mountain, "Go, throw yourself into the sea," and does not doubt in his heart but believes that what he says will happen, it will be done for him.

Therefore I tell you, whatever you ask for in prayer, believe that you have received it, and it will be yours.

Mark 11:23,24

Yet he did not waver through unbelief regarding the promise of God, but was strengthened in his faith and gave glory to God,

Being fully persuaded that God had power to do what he had promised.

Romans 4:20,21

So that your faith might not rest on men's wisdom, but on God's power.

1 Corinthians 2:5

But what does it say? "The word is near you; it is in your mouth and in your heart," that is, the word of faith we are proclaiming.

Consequently, faith comes from hearing the message, and the message is heard through the word of Christ.

Romans 10:8,17

Clearly no one is justified before God by the law, because, "The righteous will live by faith."

Galatians 3:11

In addition to all this, take up the shield of faith, with which you can extinguish all the flaming arrows of the evil one.

Ephesians 6:16

So do not throw away your confidence; it will be richly rewarded.
But my righteous one will live by faith. And if he shrinks back, I will not be pleased with him.

Hebrews 10:35,38

Now faith is being sure of what we hope for and certain of what we do not see.
And without faith it is impossible to please God, because anyone who comes to him must believe that he exists and that he rewards those who earnestly seek him.

Hebrews 11:1,6

But when he asks, he must believe and not doubt, because he who doubts is like a wave of the sea, blown and tossed by the wind.

James 1:6

For everyone born of God overcomes the world. This is the victory that has overcome the world, even our faith.

1 John 5:4

Are they not the ones who are slandering the noble name of him to whom you belong?
What good is it, my brothers, if a man claims to have faith but has no deeds? Can such faith save him?
You foolish man, do you want evidence that faith without deeds is useless?

James 2:7,14,20

❧ *When You Need To Trust God* ❧

*T*rust in the Lord with all your heart and lean not on your own understanding;

In all your ways acknowledge him, and he will make your paths straight.

Proverbs 3:5,6

My God is my rock, in whom I take refuge, my shield and the horn of my salvation. He is my stronghold, my refuge and my savior – from violent men you save me.

2 Samuel 22:3

But let all who take refuge in you be glad; let them ever sing for joy. Spread your protection over them, that those who love your name may rejoice in you.

Psalm 5:11

The Lord is my rock, my fortress and my deliverer; my God is my rock, in whom I take refuge. He is my shield and the horn of my salvation, my stronghold.

Psalm 18:2

In you I trust, O my God. Do not let me be put to shame, nor let my enemies triumph over me.

Psalm 25:2

The Lord redeems his servants; no one will be condemned who takes refuge in him.

Psalm 34:22

Trust in the Lord and do good; dwell in the land and enjoy safe pasture. Commit your way to the Lord; trust in him and he will do this.

Psalm 37:3,5

When I am afraid, I will trust in you.

In God, whose word I praise, in God I trust; I will not be afraid. What can mortal man do to me?

In God I trust; I will not be afraid. What can man do to me?

Psalm 56:3,4,11

It is better to take refuge in the Lord than to trust in man.
It is better to take refuge in the Lord than to trust in princes.

Psalm 118:8,9

Fear of man will prove to be a snare, but whoever trusts in the Lord is kept safe.

Proverbs 29:25

God is not a man, that he should lie, nor a son of man, that he should change his mind. Does he speak and then not act? Does he promise and not fulfill?

Numbers 23:19

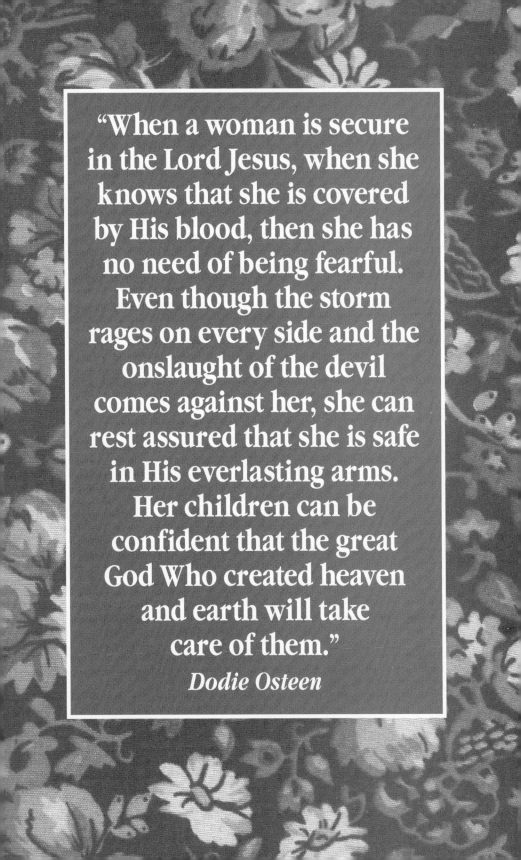

"When a woman is secure in the Lord Jesus, when she knows that she is covered by His blood, then she has no need of being fearful. Even though the storm rages on every side and the onslaught of the devil comes against her, she can rest assured that she is safe in His everlasting arms. Her children can be confident that the great God Who created heaven and earth will take care of them."

Dodie Osteen

PERSONAL PRAYERS

❧ *Prayer for Spouse* ❧

ather, I thank You for my mate who delights himself in You. Your Spirit rests upon him – the Spirit of wisdom and understanding, the Spirit of counsel and power; the Spirit of knowledge and the fear of the Lord.

Thank You, Father, that my mate is loving, patient and kind. He is not envious, boastful, proud, rude, or self-seeking. He is not easily angered and never keeps a record of my wrongs. He is quick to forgive. He rejoices when righteousness and truth prevail.

He always protects me, speaks well of me and believes the best of me. He always hopes and perseveres because You, Lord, are his primary focus.

Father, because we love You first and foremost and are submitted to You as the Head of the Church, we are committed and submitted to one another, daily maturing in the oneness You meant to exist in our relationship.

In my mate's tongue is life and not death. He strengthens our relationship by speaking Your Word, Lord, in the face of any circumstance. He is never degrading or intimidating, but always uplifts, edifies and encourages.

Thank You, Father, that my mate is a peacemaker. He refuses to allow strife, envy, or selfishness in our marriage and home. Because our home is a haven of love, peace and harmony, our prayers are not hindered and Your blessings are overtaking us, Lord.

Thank You, Father, for helping us to mature in You and in our relationship with one another. Amen.

Scripture References:

Ephesians 5:22-33
Psalm 37:41
Mark 11:23-25
Proverbs 18:21
James 3:16-18
1 Peter 3:7

Isaiah 11:2
Corinthians 13:4-8
Isaiah 1:19
Matthew 5:9
Psalm 133:1-3

❧ *Prayer for Children* ❧

*T*hank You, Father, that our children are a heritage and a reward from You. Before You formed them in the womb, You knew each child. You knit each child together in the womb fearfully and wonderfully, Lord.

Your thoughts and plans for our children are blessed. You created them to be signs and wonders in the earth.

Our children are taught of You, Lord, and great is their peace.

No weapon formed against our children shall prosper, Lord Jesus. Wrong relationships cannot prevail, because they hunger and thirst for Your righteousness, Lord. Wrong thoughts cannot prevail in our children, because they have the mind of Christ. Lies and deception cannot prosper against them or take residence in them, because they are dominated by Your truth, Lord. Greater is He who is in them than he who is in the world.

No sickness or disease can prosper against our children, Lord, because they have been redeemed from the curse of the law, and by Your stripes, Lord Jesus, they have already been healed.

It is well with our children, because they are respectful and obedient to their parents and to all who are in authority over them in Jesus' name.

Your shed blood, Lord Jesus, cleanses and protects our children – spirit, soul (which includes mind, will, emotions and intellect) and body.

Thank You, Father, that You are perfecting everything that concerns our children. They will do great exploits for You, Father, in Jesus' name. Amen.

Scripture References:

Psalm 127:3-5	Jeremiah 1:5
Psalm 139:13-18	Jeremiah 29:11
Isaiah 8:18, KJV	Isaiah 54:13,17
Proverbs 11:21	Matthew 5:6
1 Corinthians 2:161	John 4:4
Galatians 3:13,141	Peter 2:24
Ephesians 6:1-3	Psalm 138:8
Daniel 11:32b	

❧ *Prayer for Health and Healing* ❧

*W*e accept You, Father, as Jehovah Rapha, our Healer, for You said, "I am the Lord Who heals you." We accept Jesus' completed work at Calvary, which includes full payment for our sicknesses and diseases, as well as our sins, poverty and spiritual death.

For existing symptoms, sicknesses and diseases, Lord, we rise up in the authority You have invested in us and we agree with Your Word, "Nothing will harm us."

You said in Your Word, Lord, to decree a thing and it would be so. We decree that sickness and disease cannot come near our dwelling, for Your divine health resides in us, O Lord.

Father, we receive the promise of Your Word that though the righteous face many afflictions, which could include sickness, disease and/or symptoms, *You will deliver us from them all!*

Because we revere Your name, Lord Jesus, the Sun of Righteousness will arise in our behalf with healing in His wings. We will go forth totally whole, leaping as calves loosed from their stalls, with rejoicing in our hearts.

In You, Lord Jesus, we will run through enemy troops and leap over enemy walls! Nothing shall be impossible to us that is ordained of You, because we have Your vitality, Lord Jesus! We will not be hindered from fulfilling Your purposes for our lives, Lord, because we live and move and have our total being, including health and healing, in You! Amen.

Scripture References:

Job 22:28, KJV

Exodus 15:26

Luke 10:19

Psalm 34:19

Acts 17:28

Proverbs 17:22

Malachi 4:2, AMP

1 Peter 2:24

Psalm 91:10-16

Matthew 8:17

Psalm 18:29

≈ *Prayer for Finances* ≈

*H*eavenly Father, thank You that You teach us how to profit and lead us in the way we should go.

As born-again believers, Lord, we thank You that our covenant agreement with You includes provision for all of our needs. It includes an exchange of our lack for Your prosperity, Lord, not only in finances, but in every area of life.

We speak to the mountain of financial lack, Lord, and command it to be removed from our lives and replaced with the finances from heaven, which are loosed as we bring our tithes and offerings into Your storehouse. We decree financial increase, Lord, not just to bless us, but so we can bless others with the Good News of You, Lord Jesus, as well as meet their practical needs of food, clothing and shelter.

We decree that we are the head and not the tail, above and not beneath, blessed coming and going and abounding in our checking and saving accounts.

Thank You for the abundant life we have in You, Lord Jesus. We command that the devil restore seven-fold, in Jesus' name, for anything he has taken from us.

We loose the wealth of the wicked to come into our hands, Lord, so we can complete Your plans upon the earth.

Thank You, Father, that in Christ Jesus, we are prosperous in our finances, in health and in well-being, just as our soul prospers by daily input of and meditation upon Your Word, Lord. Amen.

Scripture References:

Isaiah 48:17, AMP	Philippians 4:19
Proverbs 13:22, KJV	Mark 11:23,24
Job 22:28	Deuteronomy 28:1-14
Malachi 3:8-12	Psalm 115:14,15
Psalm 41:1,2	John 10:10
3 John 2, KJV	Joshua 1:8

✇ *Prayer for Safety and Protection* ✇

*F*ather, we decree safety over our lives and over the lives of our seed (our children) – spirit, soul, body and property – because of the shed blood of Your Son, Jesus Christ.

We dwell in the shelter of the Most High and rest in His shadow. You, Lord, are our refuge and fortress, and we trust in You.

Thank You for protecting us from the devil's traps and snares, Lord, and for covering us with Your feathers. We take refuge under Your wings, and Your faithfulness is a shield to us. Thank You, Lord, that You give Your angels charge over us to keep us in all of our ways.

We will not fear, for You are not only our dwelling, but our Source of everything for our lives, Lord, including safety and protection.

It is a covenant promise to Your children, Lord, that if we love and acknowledge You, not just with lip service but from our hearts, You will protect us, deliver us, honor us and give us long life.

Thank You for the armor of protection You have given us, Lord – the belt of truth; the breastplate of righteousness; the gospel of peace for our feet; the shield of faith to extinguish all the flaming arrows of the devil; the helmet of salvation; the sword of the Spirit, which is Your Word; and prayer in the Spirit with all kinds of prayer.

We shall not be destroyed by any plot or scheme of the devil, Lord, for we are knowledgeable of Your Word. As we resist the devil with Your Word, he flees from us in great terror! Greater is He who is in us than he who is in the world.

Thank You, Lord, for divine safety and protection over our spirit, our mind, will, emotions and intellect, over our bodies and over the provision and possessions You have given us. Amen.

Scripture References:

Revelation 12:11	Job 22:28, KJV
Psalm 91:1-16	Matthew 18:19,20
Hosea 4:6	James 4:7
1 John 4:4	Ephesians 6:10-18

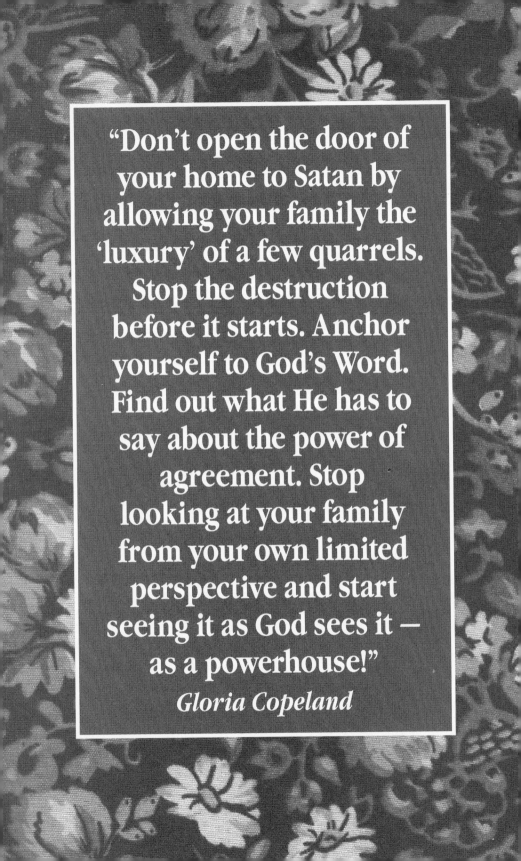

"Don't open the door of your home to Satan by allowing your family the 'luxury' of a few quarrels. Stop the destruction before it starts. Anchor yourself to God's Word. Find out what He has to say about the power of agreement. Stop looking at your family from your own limited perspective and start seeing it as God sees it — as a powerhouse!"

Gloria Copeland

HEAVEN ON EARTH

"HEAVEN ON EARTH IN YOUR HOME AND MARRIAGE"

BY
KENNETH & GLORIA COPELAND

$\mathcal{L}$iving in a home filled with the love and peace of God Himself is almost like living in heaven right here on earth.

We all know that's true. And we all long to live in such a home. Yet time and again, we shortchange our families. We spend our kindest words and our most winning smiles on those beyond our front door. Despite our best intentions, we fall prey to temptation, to selfishness, and impatience at home more often than anywhere else.

Have you ever wondered why?

The answer is simpler than you may suspect. Spiritually speaking, your family is under attack. You see, it is not only one of your most precious gifts, when it's operating in harmony, it's one of your most powerful resources. Satan knows that, even if you don't. And he's out to destroy it.

His battle plan is simple. He will do everything he can to create strife in your home. He'll stir up feelings of self-pity and jealousy. He'll encourage you to nurse resentments and harbor bitterness. And through it all, his purpose remains the same: to divide and destroy your home.

Why is he so terrified of your family living in harmony? Look at Matthew 18:19,20 (KJV) and you'll see. There Jesus says, **Again I say unto you, That if two of you shall agree on earth as touching any thing that they shall ask, it shall be done for them of my Father which is in heaven. For where two or three are gathered together in my name, there am I in the midst of them.**

When God's people get in harmony with each other, miracles start to happen. Their agreement creates an atmosphere in which God's supernatural, miracle-working power is free to flow!

So Satan is constantly tempting us to spoil that atmosphere, to foul things up by being at odds with each other. And all too often we fall prey to his tactics simply because we don't realize just how dangerous strife really is. One close look at the Word of God will solve that problem, however. It says in no uncertain terms that strife is extremely dangerous business.

Second Timothy 2:26, for example, says that those who are in strife are taken captive by Satan at his will. James 3:16 (KJV) says **where envying and strife is, there is confusion and every evil work.**

That's how many Christian families are destroyed. They allow themselves the "luxury" of a few quarrels, a few disagreements without realizing they're offering Satan an open door into their home. And before they know it, he's tearing their lives apart.

How can you stop the destruction before it starts? Anchor yourself to God's Word. Find out what He has to say about the power of agreement. Stop looking at your marriage from your own limited human perspective and start seeing it as God sees it. That way you won't drift helplessly into an argument every time a gust of emotion blows through your home.

According to the Word of God, marriage is not an arrangement based on convenience or on emotion. It's a covenant between two people, each promising to give himself to the other in life and even in death if need be. It is so serious and so sacred that the New Testament frequently compares the relationship of the husband and wife to the relationship between Jesus and the Church.

Of the relationship between Christ and the Church, Ephesians 5:30 (KJV) says, **For we are members of his body, of his flesh, and of his bones.** And of the relationship between a man and his wife, Matthew 19:5 (KJV) says, **For this cause shall a man leave father and mother, and shall cleave to his wife: and they twain shall be one flesh.**

Just as the Church has been joined with Jesus in spirit to actually become His Body on the earth, so marriage partners are joined spiritually and physically to become "one flesh." The two relationships are so similar that one version of the Bible says that by rightly discerning the Body of Christ, you rightly discern the marriage union.

Are you beginning to see how powerful God intended the marriage relationship to be?

Now look again at Matthew 18:20 (KJV). It says, **where two or three are gathered together in my name, there am I in the midst of them.** If you and your spouse are both believers, you've been joined together in Jesus' name. Isn't that right? That means Jesus is there in the midst of you. Now all you two have to do is to agree on anything according to the Word of God, ask it, and it will be done for you. Jesus said so!

You don't have to be the victim of your circumstances! You don't have to sit around and let the devil steal your kids or your health or your money. If you'll just get in agreement and pray, you can run him right out of those areas of your life.

Read Matthew 18:19 (KJV) again. **If two of you shall agree on earth as touching any thing that they shall ask, it shall be done for them of my Father which is in heaven.** Meditate on that verse. Get a revelation of it! When you do, you won't be willing to throw away that kind of prayer power for the sake of some silly argument!

You'll also want to clean out your emotional closets and get rid of all the resentments you've stored up from the past. Why? Because those, too, will sap the power of your prayers. Follow the instructions of Jesus in Mark 11:25 (KJV). **And when ye stand praying, forgive, if ye have aught against any: that your Father also which is in heaven may forgive you your trespasses.**

Gloria and I know how important harmony is within our family. We endeavor to keep the power of agreement at work in our lives. We work at not allowing strife in our home. We both realize that it's more important to keep the peace than it is to prove that we're right and that helps us keep our conversations with each other in line.

Rather than being guided by our human wisdom, we must allow ourselves to be guided by the wisdom which is from above which, according to James 3:17 (AMP), is peace-loving, courteous, considerate, gentle, willing to yield to reason, and full of compassion. When we live in peace instead of strife, we are enjoying one of God's most powerful blessings – a love-ruled home.

You may say, "But Brother Copeland, you don't know my wife! She's the one who's causing all the problems. I've been praying that God would change her for 20 years."

Don't you worry about that. You concentrate on YOU! Start praying that God will turn you into the husband of her dreams. Wives, you start asking God to make you into the wife your husband really needs. You'll be amazed at the miracles that can come out of a prayer like that.

Once you get things straight between you and your husband or you and your wife, you'll have a lot more power where your children are concerned. In this day of crime, drugs, perversion, and rebellion running rampant, Christian parents all over this nation are concerned about their children. Yet very few of them know what rights and promises are given to them as parents in the Word of God.

Galatians 3:13,14 (KJV) says, **Christ hath redeemed us from the curse of the law, being made a curse for us: for it is written, Cursed is every one that hangeth on a tree: That the blessing of Abraham might come on the Gentiles through Jesus Christ; that we might receive the promise of the Spirit through faith.** For the most part, those of us who are believers have been well taught about our redemption from sin, sickness, disease, and poverty. We know we don't have to put up with those things. But often, when it comes to our children, we live with the curse as though we had no other choice.

What are the effects of that curse? You can find them in Deuteronomy 28:32 (KJV).

Thy sons and thy daughters shall be given unto another people, and thine eye shall look, and fail with longing for them all the day long: and there shall be no might in thine hand. And verse 41 says, **Thou shalt beget sons and daughters, but thou shalt not enjoy them; for they shall go into captivity.**

Many parents today are living out these verses. They're watching helplessly as their children are taken captive by the ways of the world. But it doesn't have to be that way. Jesus has broken the power of the curse in the life of every believer. Act on His promise. Order Satan out of your children's lives.

Don't wait for your children to make the first move. Go to battle for them in prayer. Children don't understand the unseen forces that come against them. Part of your responsibility as a parent is to put up a shield of faith that will help protect your children from the influence of the evil one.

Like most parents, Gloria and I have had to deal with rebellion. We realized that it had to be stopped and stopped quickly. When we first saw the warning signs, we sought for the scriptures we could use to combat these forces. Gloria made a study of them. She wrote down every scriptural promise that she could find concerning our children.

I'll never forget the day she and I sat down in the middle of the bed amidst a pile of papers and Bibles and agreed on those scriptures in prayer. We took authority in the spirit world and refused to give the devil any room to operate.

Once we exercised the authority given us by God's Word, we also took every opportunity to minister love to the children. Before long, they were responding to it. It wasn't easy, though. At times we wanted to cry or lose our tempers. But, whenever we were tempted to react in the natural, we would remember such scriptures as Jeremiah 31:16,17 (KJV). **Thus saith the Lord; Refrain thy voice from weeping, and thine eyes from tears: for thy work shall be rewarded, saith the Lord; and they [your children] shall come again from the land of the enemy. And there is hope in thine end, saith the Lord, that thy children shall come again to their own border.**

We stood on the promises of God, and those promises got the job done! They'll do the same for you. Take them to heart. Resist the temptation to weep for your children. Start believing the Word. It is the only thing that will bring them around. Second Peter 2:9 assures us that God knows how to deliver them, so give Him the opportunity. Do your part and trust Him to do His.

And above all, **as far as it depends on you, live at peace with everyone** (Rom. 12:18, AMP). Resist strife just as you would sin or sickness. Discord is deadly, and it is always of the devil. You can't afford it. It will paralyze the power of God in your life.

If you allow the enemy to stop you at your own front door, you will be no threat to him anywhere else. Decide today that disharmony, clashing, and tension are luxuries that you cannot afford – especially at home! Give your family one of the greatest gifts of all time – a home full of love, peace, and power of God. Then you can all enjoy a little bit of heaven on earth...all year around.